W9-CCB-808

# SPILLING THE
# beans

## cooking and baking with beans and grains every day

JULIE VAN ROSENDAAL
& SUE DUNCAN

whitecap

Copyright © 2011 by Julie Van Rosendaal
and Sue Duncan
Whitecap Books

All rights reserved. No part of this publication may be
reproduced, stored in a retrieval system, or transmitted
in any form or by any means, electronic, mechanical,
photocopying, recording, or otherwise, without the prior
written permission of the publisher. For more information
contact Whitecap Books, at Suite 210, 314 West Cordova
Street, Vancouver, BC, Canada V6B 1E8.

The information in this book is true and complete to the
best of the authors' knowledge. All recommendations
are made without guarantee on the part of the authors or
Whitecap Books Ltd. The authors and publisher disclaim
any liability in connection with the use of this information.

Whitecap Books is known for its expertise in the cookbook
market, and has produced some of the most innovative
and familiar titles found in kitchens across North America.
Visit our website at www.whitecap.ca.

PUBLISHER Michael Burch
EDITOR Carolyn Stewart
DESIGNER Mauve Pagé
FOOD PHOTOGRAPHER Julie Van Rosendaal
FOOD STYLISTS Julie Van Rosendaal and Sue Duncan

PRINTED IN Canada

LIBRARY AND ARCHIVES CANADA CATALOGUING
IN PUBLICATION

Van Rosendaal, Julie, 1970-
   Spilling the beans : cooking and baking with beans
and grains every day / Julie Van Rosendaal, Sue Duncan.

Includes index.
ISBN 978-1-77050-041-9

   1. Cooking (Beans). 2. Cooking (Cereals). 3. Cooking
(Legumes).
I. Duncan, Sue, 1970- II. Title.

TX803.B4V36 2011    641.6'565    C2011-902924-3

The publisher acknowledges the financial support of
the Government of Canada through the Canada Book
Fund (CBF) and the Province of British Columbia through
the Book Publishing Tax Credit.

13 14 15    9 8 7 6

# Contents

1      Introduction

15     Beans for Breakfast

38     Appies & Snacks

65     Beany, Grainy Salads

95     Sandwiches

109    Soups & Stews

143    One-Dish Meals

183    Pasta

199    Beany Sides

208    Baking with Beans

261    Index

# INTRODUCTION

BEANS. WE KNOW THEM WELL, BUT AS familiar as they are, a huge number of us don't have a clue what to do with them once we get them home to our kitchens. Give someone a chicken or pound of ground beef and dinner ideas immediately come to mind, but the same does not seem to apply to chickpeas or lentils, particularly in their dry state. It's amazing that legumes, which have been around for centuries and are present in nearly every cuisine in the world, are still such a mystery even to skilled cooks. The process of soaking and simmering seems daunting, even though it requires less culinary skill than cooking rice or pasta.

The combination of grains and legumes is one of the oldest known culinary pairings, common in cuisines on every continent and arguably the most inexpensive source of protein on the planet. All legumes—beans, chickpeas, peas, and lentils—are high in fibre, protein, and other essential nutrients. They're low in fat, cholesterol-free, versatile, environmentally friendly, and cheap. They could very well be the world's most perfect food.

With a long shelf life (whether dry or canned), beans are the ultimate in healthy convenience food. And as people come to recognize the environmental impact of meat (a 2006 report by the United Nations Food and Agriculture Organization estimates that global livestock production is responsible for one-fifth of all greenhouse gases—more than transportation), beans have become a more environmentally savvy choice for those fighting climate change at mealtimes. A sustainable crop that's easy and inexpensive to grow and store, legumes naturally fix nitrogen in the soil, improving its fertility and reducing fertilizer costs for farmers.

As two omnivorous home cooks interested in incorporating more beans into our diets for these very reasons, we consulted each other for inspiration. We both love to spend time in the kitchen (together, whenever possible), love good food, and tend to use meat in smaller quantities, more as a condiment than the main event. Once we delved into the world of beans and learned what could be done with them, we decided to become their cheering section, to familiarize the not-so-bean-savvy with the lowly legume, and ultimately help restore its place on the dinner table.

Beans (and their good buddies, whole grains) of all kinds are good for your body, your schedule, your pocketbook, and the environment. So let's eat.

## All about Beans

NOBODY'S PERFECT, BUT IN THE FOOD world, beans are about as close as you can get.

What we refer to as beans—the legume kind rather than the green-bean kind—are actually large plant seeds. The whole young pods of bean plants, picked before the pods ripen and dry, are the green beans, broad beans, and green peas we see in produce markets. (Yes, peas are legumes, too. So are peanuts.) So there are fresh beans, and then there are the seeds from those beans that we also call beans but know as legumes or pulses as well. The term *pulse* is almost synonymous with legume but is reserved for crops harvested solely for the dry seed (yes—legumes) and so refers mostly to peas, beans, lentils, and chickpeas, leaving soybeans and peanuts out. Clear as mud?

So—the beans we're talking about here are legumes and pulses. Are you still with us?

There are hundreds of varieties out there, the most common being red and white kidney beans (the latter are also called cannellini), black beans, all manner of little white beans (including navy and Great Northern), chickpeas, and lentils. But you'll come across dry beans of all sizes and colours and it doesn't much matter whether or not you can identify them—they're treated more or less the same in the kitchen, and can most often be shuffled from recipe to recipe. If you can cook one kind, you can cook them all.

Although the specific profile of each type of legume varies slightly, all are nutritionally stellar. Beans are high in fibre and protein, low in fat, cholesterol-free, and nutrient-dense—rich in B vitamins, iron, niacin, and folate. Most contain soluble fibre, which has been shown to help reduce blood cholesterol levels. Some studies have shown legume consumption correlates with a reduced risk of death from heart disease.

Eating a well-balanced diet of both beans and grains can also help your body get protein. Most vegetables contain protein in varying amounts—beans and lentils are quite high in that department, as are many grains and nuts—but vegetable protein sources are often deficient in one or more of the essential amino acids. Fortunately, legumes are rich in the amino acid that most grains lack, and vice versa. Isn't that handy? In general terms, when different sources of protein (whether meat, legumes, dairy, nuts, or grains) are combined in the diet, they will enhance each other's absorbability. By eating a varied diet, we can reduce or cancel out the deficiencies of an individual food source. To learn more about proteins and essential amino acids, see A Word From the Doctor on page 7.

There are so many good reasons beans are

a large part of virtually every cuisine around the globe, but we North Americans are lagging behind. So really, we should all get to know them a little better—particularly in our kitchens and around our dinner tables.

## Types of Beans

### CANNED OR DRY?

We use both canned and dry beans, and most of the recipes in this book can be made with either (with the exception of some of the baked goods, for reasons explained below). Nutritionally, canned and dry beans are virtually the same, their biggest differences being texture and sodium content. The sludge that canned beans arrive in can be high in sodium, but you can get rid of much of it by rinsing and draining them well.

Canned beans and lentils are unfailingly quick and convenient. They store well, and are therefore easy to keep on hand. They are also softer, which can come in handy if you want to purée them until they're perfectly smooth (read: undetectable) to add to baked goods such as cupcakes and pizza dough.

Dry beans are usually even less expensive than the canned varieties, and although it takes a little more time to get a dry bean to the table, it requires very little effort. When cooking dry beans and lentils, keep in mind that their cooked volume will vary a little. Lentils and chickpeas will expand to approximately 3 times their dry volume once cooked; most other varieties of beans expand to about 2 to 3 times their dry volume. We usually cook extra and then freeze whatever we don't need immediately. Check page 6 for more information on how to cook your beans. Or just keep the can opener handy!

The whole concept of protein combining was introduced by Frances Moore Lappé in her 1971 book *Diet for a Small Planet*. At the time, it was assumed that in order to achieve a perfect balance of amino acids in a vegetarian diet it was necessary to eat grains and legumes in the same bowl. This was later debunked as a theory and retracted by the author, but many modern sources still endorse this concept. In practice, getting a sufficiency of complete protein in our diets takes very little time or effort so long as we eat a variety of nutritious foods daily. When we introduce more legumes in our diets—adding a beany salad at lunch or some roasted chickpeas before dinner, for instance—they match up very nicely with the grains that are most often already there (think toast or oatmeal in the mornings, bread with lunch, rice with dinner). In other words, we can supply those different amino acids at different times of the day, and our bodies still get the benefits!

## A Word about Flatulence

SO YOU WANT TO EAT MORE BEANS and lentils, but you're concerned about the toots. There are quite a few theories out there on how to reduce gaseous side effects, and different things seem to work for different people.

After soaking dry beans, try changing the water before cooking them. Once they are cooked, rinse them thoroughly and discard the water. This is said to help break down the oligosaccharides that are responsible for the reputation beans have as the musical fruit. If you're using canned beans, drain and rinse them well.

If beans aren't a regular part of your diet, introduce them gradually—eating small quantities of beans and lentils frequently (as opposed to large quantities infrequently) may allow your digestive system to adapt. If your

BLACK-EYED PEAS

CHICKPEAS

DU PUY LENT

LITTLE WHITE BEANS

LIMA BEANS

MIXED BEA

SOYBEANS

GREEN/BROW
LENTI

PINTO BEANS

RED KIDNEY BEANS

TURTLE BEA

YELLOW SPLIT PEAS

RED LENTILS

BARLEY

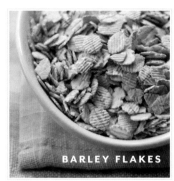

BARLEY FLAKES

BROWN RICE PASTA

QUINOA

BULGUR

COUSCOUS

LONG-GRAIN BROWN & WILD RICE

LONG-GRAIN WHITE RICE

ROLLED OATS

SHORT-GRAIN BROWN RICE

SHORT-GRAIN RICE

WILD RICE

STEEL-CUT OATS

SOBA NOODLES

WHEAT BERRIES

YELLOW CORNMEAL

meals have seldom included beans in the past, it's probably a good idea not to jump in too enthusiastically right off the bat.

Some people swear by certain herbs and spices cooked with the beans: cumin, coriander, turmeric, fennel seed, bay leaf, and asafoetida (common in Indian cooking and also known as *hing*) are all reputed to reduce gaseous side effects. (Our recipes don't call for asafoetida because it can be difficult to find—if you do have some, use it sparingly, and cook it briefly in oil or butter before adding it to the main ingredients.) We've also heard that a pinch of baking soda or a strip of kombu (a type of seaweed) cooked with the beans can help, but we haven't noticed a difference ourselves. Of course, we're big fans of beans and as such, they tend to love us back.

If after eating beans you do let 'er rip more often than you're used to (not to suggest that you ever did such a thing in the past), feel free to blame us. Use all our health and environmental pro-bean arguments. Or shuffle around and find a squeak in the chair or floorboard to blame it on. Or go stand next to the dog. And don't give up on beans—eat more of them. The rhyme "beans, beans, the musical fruit / the more you eat, the more you toot / the more you toot, the better you feel / so let's have beans at every meal!" isn't entirely accurate . . . it should go, "the more you eat, the *less* you toot," but we wholeheartedly agree with the "feeling better" and "every meal" parts.

## How to Cook a Bean

OK, LET'S TALK ABOUT COOKING DRY beans. All this presoaking and cooking hysteria? It's really not that big a deal. All you need to do is boil them until they're tender—that's really about it. If you want to presoak them, do. If you didn't think that far ahead, don't sweat it.

Dry beans are most often presoaked (soaked before cooking) to get a jump start on the hydration process, shortening their cooking time. Lentils are the exception to the rule—there's no need to soak lentils before cooking them, which makes it easy to toss a handful into a pot of soup or stew. There's technically no need to presoak any other beans before cooking them, either—if you don't have time, expect to add another 30 minutes or so to your cooking time—but if you think of it, covering a handful of beans with water before you go to bed or leave for work in the morning will save you some time later. (Bonus: soaking is believed to reduce their flatulent effect. It's worth a try.)

Smaller varieties of beans cook much more quickly than larger varieties, and older beans—those that have been stored longer (whether before or after purchase)—will take a little longer to cook.

No matter what variety of dry beans you're cooking—white beans, black beans, kidney beans, chickpeas—the process is the same. Sort through them quickly in case there are any small pebbles among them (pretty rare, but it happens), and if you're going to presoak them, do: cover them with water by at least 2 inches (you'll be amazed how much they swell) and let them sit for 6 to 8 hours or thereabouts. Don't worry if they sit for more or less time.

The quick-soak method will shorten your soaking time: cover your beans with plenty of water, bring them to a boil, uncovered, then take them off the heat and set aside for an hour or two. (This plumps them up more

# A WORD FROM THE DOCTOR
## *(who is also Julie's dad)*

### ABOUT FIBRE

Fibre is a form of carbohydrate and carbohydrates are an important source of the energy we need for our bodies (particularly our brains) to function. Think of carbohydrates as Lego—similar blocks of a few colours stuck together in different configurations, some as simple constructions, some as very complex ones. These building blocks are called simple sugars and we can only get the energy they contain when they are separated—when the foods we eat are broken down to their component parts.

Now also imagine that some blocks have been stuck together tightly and are difficult to separate; others have been glued together and are impossible to separate. The difficult-to-take-apart constructions represent complex carbohydrates. Among these, the ones that are particularly difficult or impossible to break down are fibres.

The upper bowel, or small intestine, is very good at absorbing individual building blocks (sugars) into the body. Foods that contain large quantities of sugars have a high glycemic index. Such foods are not as healthy as those in which carbohydrates occur in more complex forms. When the building blocks are stuck together, the body must break them down into a simpler form, to digest them, so they can be absorbed. This takes time, so the impact of a sugar load is reduced when carbohydrates are eaten in this form. Eating complex carbs is a much healthier way to get one's energy than eating simple sugars, also known as refined carbohydrates. Fruits, vegetables, beans, and grains are foods in which much of the carbohydrate content occurs in the complex form.

The human body has a limited ability to digest some of the more complex fibres. This varies with the food involved. When complex carbohydrate (fibre), can't be broken down and absorbed, it passes through the small intestine into the large intestine, or colon. The large numbers of bacteria that live in the colon are able to digest some of the complex carbs that we cannot. In doing so they produce byproducts, some of which are gases.

The food we eat contains a wide range of fibres that vary in the way they affect and benefit us. In general we group these fibres as either soluble or insoluble. Soluble fibre, found in foods such as beans and oatmeal, tends to reduce the levels of cholesterol in the blood and so helps reduce the risk of heart or cardiovascular disease. Insoluble fibre, found in large quantities in vegetables and unrefined grains, produces the bulk to keep things moving through our colons. Both are important, but for different reasons.

### ABOUT PROTEIN

Protein, an essential part of our diet, is like carbohydrate in that it consists of chains of basic building blocks that must be disassembled, absorbed into the body, and then reassembled to make the components that are critical to the growth, operation, and repair of our bodies. But the protein story is more complicated—a larger range of building blocks is needed for protein synthesis. These blocks are the amino acids.

To further complicate matters, the body needs a large number of proteins and each has its own complex formula of amino acids that must be arranged in just the right way. The body needs about 20 different amino acids and it can CONTINUED . . .

produce all but 8 of them. Therefore these 8 must be included in the diet. These are the essential amino acids.

Proteins that contain all of the essential amino acids, in the proportions in which the body needs them, are said to be high-quality proteins. Foods that contain such ideal proportions of the key amino acids include egg white, meat, fish, dairy products, and soy. Foods that contain most but not all of the essential amino acids—such as beans—can be combined with other foods to fill in the gaps. Classical examples of foods that complement each other to provide the right mix of essential amino acids are beans, nuts, or lentils combined with grains. The body has some ability to store amino acids, so you don't need to eat these foods in combination at every meal. Foods containing lower-quality protein can also serve as supplements to expand the benefits of foods that contain high-quality proteins. You can get by with smaller amounts of meat, fish, and dairy products if you supplement these foods with grains, nuts, lentils, and beans. So, while an understanding of protein sources is essential for anyone eating a strictly vegetarian diet, it is also useful for anyone wishing to improve the healthfulness of their diet.

quickly, but yes, you still have to cook them.)

When you're ready to cook your beans, drain off the soaking liquid and cover them with fresh water by at least 2 inches—your bean-to-water ratio should be about 1:3. If you're concerned with retaining the nutrients from the cooking water and don't want to drain it off, keep the water to a minimum so that the beans soak up almost precisely the water they need, leaving little in the pan. What's left can go into your finished dish, unless your beans need to be drained first. (This is the way Sue does it.) If you figure you're going to drain them anyway and don't want to monitor the stove, use more water than you think you'll need, ensuring the pot won't boil dry and burn your beans. This way you can forget to check on the beans and it won't be a total disaster. (This is the way Julie does it.) Never add salt to your cooking water at the outset as it can make your beans tough, but feel free to add a clove of garlic, a few black peppercorns, a sprig of rosemary or thyme, or a bay leaf to boost flavour. Most cooks season their beans with salt halfway through or at the end of the cooking time.

Unlike rice or pasta, dry beans don't require a precise cooking time—you can go about doing your thing and stop at the stove once in a while to see if your beans are tender. Bring the beans and water to a boil, reduce the heat, and simmer uncovered. Presoaked beans typically cook in 1 to 3 hours, depending on their size, age, and density/dryness (the latter two qualities being a bit difficult to determine by sight). Although dry beans last almost indefinitely, the older they are, the longer they take to cook. The average bean takes an hour to get tender, but give yourself extra time—you never know when you'll need it. Elevation can be a factor in boiling times— at higher elevations, cooking beans can take slightly longer. Test the beans once in a while, and when they're done to your liking, take them off the heat. (If you plan to simmer them again in another recipe—baked beans, for example—you can take them off when they still have a bit of firmness to them.) Let the beans cool in their cooking liquid, if you have time, to prevent the skins from splitting.

There's also the option to cook dry beans in the slow cooker, with no need to presoak: cover them with plenty of water and cook on low for 6 to 8 hours, until tender. Resist the urge to lift the lid and check on them constantly—each time you do you release the heat, and add about 20 minutes to the cooking time.

In contrast to other dry legumes (chickpeas, kidney beans, black beans, white beans), lentils, which are far smaller in size, don't require soaking before cooking and cook in a fraction of the time—toss them in dry and they'll generally take 30 to 40 minutes. There's a huge range of lentils available, and most of the green-blue-brown varieties are interchangeable. Red lentils (often more orange-pink in colour) are an exception in that they're split with the hull removed, and so cook in very little time—about 10 or 15 minutes. (If you look closely at a red lentil you'll notice it's been split in half crosswise, which explains the shorter cooking time.) Lentils need a little less water, too; a ratio of 1:2 works fine.

Once cooked, your beans, chickpeas, or lentils can be stored in their cooking liquid in the refrigerator for up to a week, and they also freeze very well. We like to cook dry beans a little ahead of time—the day before we're planning to eat them, or earlier the same day. If you eat beans regularly, it's simple to simmer a pot whenever you have time, and then divvy them up into freezer bags or plastic containers, using the cooled cooking liquid as a sort of insulation against freezer burn. Stored this way, they'll keep nicely in the freezer for up to 6 months and thaw quickly when you need them. (To speed things up, place the bag or container in a bowl of warm water to thaw.)

## How to Cook a Grain

SO WE'VE HAD THE BIG TALK ABOUT beans—now we need to focus on the grainy part. But don't sweat it, this is pretty easy.

As we mentioned earlier, the beans–grains pairing is one of the oldest and most widespread culinary combinations in the world. Beans and grains complete each other, at least from a protein perspective, and most bean dishes pair naturally with a grain component. Think baked beans on toast, red beans and rice, hummus and pita, curry and couscous, soup with bread. The best bit is, the grain component doesn't even need to be eaten at the same meal to be beneficial. Our bodies can store the nutrients in grains (and beans) for a short time, which means if you have a bowl of oatmeal or toast in the morning and a three-bean salad at lunch, you're still off to the races.

Grains eaten in a whole, or closer to whole, state provide us with more vitamins, minerals, phytochemicals (natural plant compounds), protein, and fibre than those that are refined. Whole grains contain all parts of the grain: the bran (the outer layer, rich in fibre), the endosperm (the middle), and the germ (the nutrient-rich inner part). When grains are refined, the bran and germ portions are removed, leaving only the endosperm.

Most of us eat a lot of grain products on a daily basis already, but need to consciously extend our grain consumption beyond just wheat (and refined "white" wheat at that). A greater spectrum provides nutritional

You'll see a lot of salads in this book made with whole grains, stews that want to nestle over rice or barley, and soups that incorporate grains and pastas or that are served over rice. One grain can often be easily substituted for another—and we fully encourage you to do a little grain swapping. Check out the grain bios below, and please be aware that whole grains don't always behave with perfect predictability when it comes to water needed and cooking times. It's still easy, though—you'll soon get the hang of it.

insurance for us, and a better ecological and economic diversity for the planet.

We know we need to eat more whole grains, but for many of us our palates and culinary skills lag behind our nutritional savvy. Give yourself a break, and remember change is best achieved slowly. It's important to enjoy our food, and there's little to be gained in making eating (or cooking) a chore.

Most of the grains we use—whether they're whole, rolled, or cut—can be stored for a year or even quite a bit more, so long as they're kept perfectly dry and in an airtight container. It's a good idea to buy whenever possible from a store with a high turnover, and to buy in smaller quantities so as to keep your own grain supply turning over. Check that stored grains smell fresh or have very little scent, with no traces of mustiness (especially if you live in a damp climate). If you live in an especially hot climate, grains can also be stored well-wrapped and sealed in the freezer, though we seldom find that necessary in our parts of the world.

### BARLEY

Most of the barley we consume at the dinner table is either pearl (or pearled) or pot barley—both are polished, meaning the bran of the whole kernel has been partially removed. Pot barley (also called Scotch barley) is a little less polished, leaving slightly more fibre than pearl barley has. At health food stores you may also find hulled barley, which is a little more hard-core—it's an entire kernel of grain with only the outer husk removed. You can also buy rolled barley flakes, which look and taste just like rolled oats (with more than twice the fibre), and barley flour.

Cook pearl or pot barley uncovered in about triple its volume of water (as you would cook pasta) for 40 to 45 minutes, then drain well. Rolled barley flakes can be used almost anywhere you would use old-fashioned rolled oats (expect a little more chew), and will cook on their own in about 20 minutes. Barley flour is great in muffins and pancakes, but is quite heavy—substitute small amounts at a time.

## BULGUR

Not actually a grain itself, bulgur is a whole-grain cereal made most often from durum wheat and usually sold parboiled. It comes in different sizes; the coarser the bulgur the longer it will take to become tender. (It's often confused with cracked wheat, which is the cracked whole wheat grain that has not been parboiled. Big difference!) Sort of a heartier version of couscous, it can be swapped for it in most recipes.

Cook bulgur by soaking it in cold water for 20 to 30 minutes (at a ratio of 1 part bulgur to 1½ parts water), until tender, and then draining and squeezing the excess water out with your hands. You can also prepare it as you would couscous (see below), using 1½ times the volume of water to bulgur.

## COUSCOUS

Not a grain in its own right, but actually a tiny nubbin of wheat pasta, couscous can be made of white or whole wheat semolina—a coarsely ground durum wheat.

To prepare, put 1 cup (250 mL) couscous in a bowl and pour 1¼ cups (310 mL) boiling water overtop; cover and let sit about 10 minutes, then fluff with a fork. How easy is that?

## OATS

A Scottish classic, oats are sold most often as rolled flakes, but can also be found in the form of steel-cut oats—whole-grain groats (the inner portion of the oat kernel) that have been cut into 2 or 3 pieces rather than being rolled. When we call for oats in this book, we're referring to either old-fashioned rolled oats or quick oats, the difference being the size of the rolled flake. Old-fashioned (or large-flake oats) are whole oats rolled out into flake form, and quick oats have been further

fragmented, allowing them to cook more quickly. (Nutritionally, they are the same.) Instant oatmeal is unsuitable for baking as it tends to become gluey and gummy.

Cook old-fashioned or quick oats uncovered in double their volume of water—old-fashioned oats will cook in about 10 minutes; quick oats in about 3. Steel-cut oats need about three times their volume in water, and take closer to 30 minutes to cook. Use oat flour in your baking (or pancakes) if you wish, keeping in mind that it doesn't contain gluten and so won't give baked goods the structure that wheat flour provides. (If you're cooking gluten-free, note that oats can often be contaminated with gluten, so ensure it says gluten-free on the package.)

## QUINOA

Pronounced *KEEN-wah*, quinoa is actually a South American seed related to beets and spinach, but it is treated as a grain in the kitchen. Quinoa, which is most commonly off-white, but often comes in shades of red and black, is one of the few grains that contains a balanced set of essential amino acids, providing a complete protein by itself. (In fact, the World Health Organization claims that quinoa contains a better protein balance than any grain, being at least equal to milk in terms of protein quality.) It's gluten-free and high in fibre, and its mild, nutty flavour lends itself well to soups, hot breakfast cereals, or anything you'd use rice or couscous for.

To prepare quinoa, you must first rinse the grain very well in cold water to remove the bitter saponins, a natural coating that wards off insects. (If you buy the grain boxed, check the package—it may already have been done for you.) Cook quinoa uncovered in plenty of water (just like you'd cook pasta) for about

a starchy seed, rather than a grain. Like quinoa, it's gluten-free and provides a complete source of protein. In this book our use of buckwheat is limited to soba noodles, but roasted buckwheat (also known as kasha) and whole buckwheat groats can be cooked as a hot cereal or side dish. You'll also come across buckwheat flour, which is grey in colour and often used for making pancakes and crêpes.

Cook buckwheat (or kasha) uncovered in double its volume of water for 15 minutes, or until tender. Drain well. Cook dry soba noodles as you would regular wheat pasta, but be aware that they cook much faster, in about 4 to 6 minutes. Check the package to be on the safe side.

### WHEAT BERRIES

A whole kernel of wheat, a wheat berry is as "whole" as wheat gets. They come in both soft and hard varieties and range from tan to dark red-brown in colour. They are deliciously nutty, hold their shape even better than brown rice, and work well as a simple side dish or breakfast cereal.

Presoak and cook wheat berries as you would cook beans—cover with water and soak overnight (or use the quick-soak method on page 6), then drain, cover with water by a few inches, bring to a boil, and simmer uncovered for about 40 minutes, until tender. Drain well.

### BROWN RICE

With the bran and germ still intact, brown rice is more fibre-rich and nutrient-dense than white rice. You'll find both short- and long-grain varieties—short-grain rice is slightly sticky, as it releases some of its starch into the water; long-grain rice will be a little more separate. (Choose short-grain rice for

15 minutes, until it's tender but still firm to the bite and the germ separates from the rest of the seed, making it look like a curly Q. Drain well in a fine sieve, return to the pot (off the heat), cover with a tea towel and then with the lid, and let it steam—this will produce fluffy quinoa—until cooled. Alternatively, cook quinoa like you would cook rice, in double its volume of water; cover and simmer on low for 15 to 18 minutes, until tender.

### BUCKWHEAT

Despite its name, buckwheat is not a variety of wheat, nor is it even related; it's actually

Introduction

risottos, rice puddings, and sushi; long-grain rice for fried rice, pilafs, and as an accompaniment to curries and such.)

To cook brown rice, bring double its volume of water to a boil (e.g., 2 cups water per 1 cup brown rice); add the rice, turn the heat to low, cover, and simmer without peeking or stirring for 40 to 45 minutes, until tender. (Lifting the lid will release heat and moisture; stirring encourages the rice to release its starch, making it sticky.) Add a little more water if it's dry but not quite cooked, or drain off any excess if that's an issue. After 45 minutes you should see tunnels through the rice, and all the liquid should be absorbed. If you like, fluff it with a fork, cover again, and set aside for 5 more minutes for fluffier rice.

Brown rice is also made into pasta; brown rice pasta tends to have a smoother mouthfeel than whole wheat pasta. Cook brown rice pasta as you would wheat pasta, being sure to use plenty of water as the pasta gives off a lot of starch as it cooks.

### WILD RICE

Actually a type of grass that grows in shallow water in North America, wild rice has an elegant appearance and a nutty flavour. It's also pretty expensive, so is often stretched by blending with brown rice.

Wild rice can vary significantly in length and colour, and also in cooking time. Cook it uncovered in plenty of water (as you would cook pasta) for 40 to 45 minutes, and drain well when it's done. The grains will often split and curl as they cook, but not all at once. The split grains will be softer; the whole ones will have a chewier texture. Because its cooking time is so similar to that of brown rice and barley, they can be cooked in the same pot together.

## Beans for Breakfast

# PANCAKES

MAKES 8 TO 12 PANCAKES, DEPENDING ON THEIR SIZE.

2 cups (500 mL) all-purpose or whole wheat flour, or a combination
2 tsp (10 mL) baking powder
Shake of ground cinnamon (optional)

Pinch of salt
1 cup (250 mL) rinsed and drained canned white beans (half a 19 oz/540 mL can)
2 cups (500 mL) milk

2 large eggs
2 Tbsp (30 mL) canola, olive, or flax oil
Berries or sliced banana (optional)

THE GREAT THING about pancakes (besides the obvious fact that they are a delicious vehicle for maple syrup) is that a) kids will eat them, and b) you can sneak a ton of good stuff into them and they'll still eat them, just by virtue of the fact that they're pancakes.

Try using different whole-grain flours in this recipe—oat, barley, quinoa, buckwheat, and brown rice flours are good choices—or add quick-cooking oats or ground flaxseed. Any combination will work, provided you keep about 1 cup of wheat flour, which provides gluten to hold the pancakes together. Puréed beans—no one will know they're there—boost nutrients and fibre.

In a large bowl, stir together the flour, baking powder, ground cinnamon (if using), and salt. In the bowl of a food processor, combine the beans with the milk, eggs, and oil and pulse until well blended. Purée until it's as smooth as you can get it.

Add the wet ingredients to the dry ingredients and whisk just until combined; don't worry about getting all the lumps out.

Preheat a heavy skillet over medium heat and spray it with non-stick cooking spray or rub it with oil (use a paper towel). Ladle the batter into the skillet, making pancakes any size you like.

Place berries or slices of banana directly onto the batter, if you're adding them. Turn the heat down a little and cook for 2 to 4 minutes, until the bottom is golden and bubbles begin to appear on the surface. Use a thin, flat spatula to flip them over and cook for another minute on the other side, until golden.

Repeat with the remaining batter. If you want everyone to eat at the same time, keep the finished pancakes warm, uncovered, in a 200°F oven.

Beans for Breakfast

# BUTTERMILK WAFFLES

## MAKES ABOUT 6 BIG BELGIAN-STYLE WAFFLES.

1 cup (250 mL) all-purpose or
  whole wheat flour
¼ cup (60 mL) cornstarch
1 Tbsp (15 mL) sugar
½ tsp (2.5 mL) baking powder

¼ tsp (1 mL) baking soda
¼ tsp (1 mL) salt
1 cup (250 mL) rinsed and
  drained canned white beans
  (half a 19 oz/540 mL can)

1½ cups (375 mL) buttermilk
¼ cup (60 mL) canola oil
1 large egg
1 tsp (5 mL) vanilla

WEEKENDS WERE MADE for waffles. As were sleepovers, and leisurely family brunches. These are easy to stir together (no need to whip the egg whites—not something we're generally up for so soon after waking up) and no one will have a clue that you've smuggled beans into them. Leftovers can be frozen and reheated in the toaster or packed in kids' lunches to eat by hand. To boost fibre and nutrients even further, add a spoonful of ground flaxseed to the dry ingredients.

In a medium bowl, stir together the flour, cornstarch, sugar, baking powder, baking soda, and salt.

In the bowl of a food processor, purée the beans with ½ cup of the buttermilk and the oil, egg, and vanilla until smooth. Add to the dry ingredients along with the remaining cup of buttermilk and whisk just until combined.

Spray your waffle maker with non-stick cooking spray, preheat it, and cook the batter according to your machine's specifications. Serve immediately or keep warm, uncovered, in a 200°F oven.

Beans for Breakfast

# MORNING GLORY
## *Muffins*
MAKES ABOUT 1½ DOZEN MUFFINS.

⅓ cup (80 mL) dry red lentils

1 cup (250 mL) all-purpose
flour

1 cup (250 mL) whole
wheat flour

¾ cup (185 mL) sugar
(white or brown)

2 tsp (10 mL) ground cinnamon

2 tsp (10 mL) baking soda

¼ tsp (1 mL) salt

2 cups (500 mL) grated carrots,
sweet potatoes, zucchini,
or a combination

½ cup (125 mL) raisins or other
dried fruit

½ cup (125 mL) chopped
pecans or walnuts (optional)

¼ cup (60 mL) flaked coconut
(optional)

1 cup (250 mL) buttermilk

½ cup (125 mL) canola oil

2 large eggs

2 tsp (10 mL) vanilla

1 apple, coarsely grated (don't
bother peeling it)

MORNING GLORY muffins are dense and nubbly by nature, making them perfect candidates for the addition of soft cooked red lentils. If you'd rather go the canned bean route, purée a cup (half a 19 oz/540 mL can) of rinsed and drained brown lentils or white beans with the buttermilk, oil, and eggs before adding them to the dry ingredients. (Leave out the dry red lentils, unless you really want to go to town with a double whammy of beans.)

Preheat the oven to 350°F. Spray muffin cups with non-stick cooking spray or line them with paper liners.

In a small saucepan, cover the lentils with water and bring to a boil; simmer for 15 minutes, or until soft. Drain well.

In a large bowl, stir together the flours, sugar, ground cinnamon, baking soda, and salt. Add the carrots, raisins, pecans, and coconut (if using) and toss to combine well.

In a small bowl, stir together the buttermilk, oil, eggs, and vanilla. Add to the carrot mixture, along with the lentils and grated apple, and stir just until the batter is combined. Don't worry about getting all the lumps out—overmixing will make your muffins tough.

Fill the muffin cups almost to the top and bake in the middle of the oven for 25 to 30 minutes, until the muffins have risen and the tops are springy to the touch. Loosen the muffins and tip them on an angle in the cups to release steam and help them cool.

Beans for Breakfast

# CRANBERRY CORNMEAL
## *Mini Muffins*
### MAKES 2 DOZEN MINI MUFFINS.

⅓ cup (80 mL) honey
¼ cup (60 mL) butter
¾ cup (185 mL) cornmeal
1 cup + 2 Tbsp (280 mL) all-purpose or whole wheat flour

¾ cup (185 mL) Candied Lentil Meal (see page 260)
1 Tbsp (15 mL) baking powder
¼ tsp (1 mL) salt

⅔ cup (160 mL) milk
1 large egg, lightly beaten
1 cup (250 mL) fresh or frozen cranberries

MINI MUFFINS ARE A great tool when your aim is to increase the graininess and overall nutrition of your baking. The size of them overcomes the problem of having a too-heavy batter, and these bake up light with crisp edges. They'll do you proud at a brunch buffet, and any leftovers are a welcome surprise in a packed lunch.

Preheat the oven to 350°F.

Measure the honey and butter into a small metal bowl or ovenproof saucepan. Place in the oven to melt for 5 to 8 minutes. Remove and set aside to cool slightly.

In a medium bowl, whisk together the cornmeal, flour, lentil meal, baking powder, and salt. Add the milk and beaten egg to the melted butter and honey and mix well. Add the honey mixture to the dry ingredients and stir gently until nearly combined. It will look soupy at first, but the cornmeal will absorb more moisture. Add the cranberries and stir until just blended.

Spray a 24-cup mini muffin pan with non-stick cooking spray (or do 12 at a time) and fill them three-quarters full with batter. Bake until the muffins are golden brown and a toothpick inserted in one of the inner muffins comes out clean of raw batter, 13 to 16 minutes. Let cool in the pan for 5 minutes, and then turn out onto a wire rack, running a thin knife around the edges to loosen the muffins if you need to.

# STICKY CINNAMON BUNS

MAKES 2 DOZEN CINNAMON BUNS.

**DOUGH:**
1 Tbsp (15 mL) active dry yeast
1 Tbsp (15 mL) sugar
2 cups (500 mL) rinsed and
    drained canned white beans
    (19 oz/540 mL can)
½ cup (125 mL) milk, warmed
¼ cup (60 mL) butter, softened
2 large eggs

4½ to 5 cups (1.125 to 1.25 L)
    all-purpose or whole wheat
    flour, or a combination, plus
    extra if needed
1 tsp (5 mL) salt

**FILLING:**
2 Tbsp (30 mL) butter, melted
1 cup (250 mL) packed brown
    sugar

1 Tbsp (15 mL) ground
    cinnamon

**GOO (OPTIONAL):**
½ cup (125 mL) brown sugar
¼ cup (60 mL) butter, melted
¼ cup (60 mL) honey, golden
    syrup, or maple syrup
¼ cup (60 mL) water

THERE'S NOTHING like a warm, chewy, yeasty cinnamon bun straight from the oven. Puréed white kidney beans add fibre, protein, and nutrients while maintaining the flavour and texture of white bread. If you do want to boost graininess, use whole wheat flour in place of all or part of the all-purpose flour, or add a spoonful of ground flaxseed. You can also scatter chopped pecans or raisins over the dough before rolling it up.

TO MAKE THE DOUGH: put 1 cup of warm water into a large bowl and add the yeast and a big pinch of the sugar; let it sit for 5 minutes, until it gets foamy. (If it does nothing, the yeast is inactive; toss it out and buy some fresh yeast!)

Meanwhile, purée the beans with the milk, butter, and eggs in a food processor, pulsing until well blended and smooth. Add to the yeast mixture along with about 3 cups of the flour, the remaining sugar, and the salt; stir (or mix with the dough hook on your stand mixer) until well blended. Add the remaining flour ½ cup at a time until you have a soft, sticky dough; turn out onto a floured surface and knead until it's soft, smooth, and elastic. Return it to the bowl, cover with a tea towel, and let rest for about an hour, until doubled in size.

On a lightly floured countertop, divide the dough in half and roll each piece into a roughly 14-inch square. Brush

CONTINUED . . .

each piece with butter and sprinkle each with ½ cup brown sugar and as much cinnamon as you like (if you want the cinnamon very evenly distributed, stir it into the brown sugar first). Roll each piece of dough up jelly roll–style.

Using a sharp serrated knife or dental floss, cut each roll in half crosswise. Cut each half in half again, and then cut each quarter into thirds. (Doing it this way is far easier than eyeballing 12 even slices, starting at one end.)

Get out two 9- × 13-inch pans or 12-cup muffin pans, or one of each, and spray them with non-stick cooking spray. Stir together the goo ingredients (if using) and divide between the bottoms of your prepared pans, or put a small spoonful into the bottom of each muffin cup.

Divide the slices of cinnamon bun among your pans, placing 4 rows of 3 in a 9- × 13-inch pan, or dropping 1 into each muffin cup. Cover with a tea towel or plastic wrap and let rise for another 30 minutes.

Preheat the oven to 350°F.

Bake for 20 to 30 minutes, until golden. If you like, drizzle with icing sugar thinned with a little water or milk to a drizzling consistency.

**NOTE:**
If you want to make them in advance and have them ready to slide into the oven first thing in the morning, cover the cut, unbaked buns and refrigerate overnight— the cold will slow the rise.

# BLACK BEAN
## *Breakfast Burritos*
### SERVES 4.

Four 10-inch (25 cm) flour
   tortillas (any kind)
Canola or olive oil, for cooking
1 small onion, finely chopped
1 small thin-skinned potato
   (Yukon Gold or red),
   coarsely grated

1½ cups (375 mL) cooked black
   beans, or a 14 oz (398 mL)
   can, rinsed and drained
⅓ cup (80 mL) salsa
1 tsp (5 mL) chili powder
Salt and pepper to taste
4 to 6 large eggs

½ cup (125 mL) shredded
   cheddar or Monterey Jack
   or crumbled feta cheese
1 avocado, sliced, or ½ cup
   (125 mL) guacamole
Fresh cilantro (optional)
Sour cream and extra salsa,
   for serving

SPICY BLACK BEAN
and scrambled egg burritos
aren't just for breakfast—
these can be repurposed
for a fast, inexpensive dinner, too. Chopped red
pepper or corn would go
well in these, as would a
crumbled chorizo sau-
sage, sautéed along with
the onion. Wrapped up in
its own package, a burrito
makes a great meal to go.

If you like, wrap your tortillas in foil and put them in a
300°F oven to warm as you make your filling. In a heavy
skillet, heat a drizzle of oil over medium-high heat. Sauté
the onion and potato for about 5 minutes, until soft and
starting to turn golden. Add the beans, salsa, chili powder,
and salt and pepper and cook for a few more minutes,
slightly smushing some of the beans with the back of your
spoon, until heated through.

Transfer the mixture to a bowl or push it aside in the skillet,
add a little more oil, and crack in the eggs. Stir the eggs
around with a spoon or spatula to scramble them.

Divide the bean mixture among the warmed tortillas,
spreading it down the middle and leaving space on the sides
and at both ends. Top with scrambled egg, cheese, avocado
or guacamole, and some fresh cilantro (if using). Fold over
one long side to cover, fold over both short ends, then roll
the whole thing over to close up into a package. Serve warm,
with extra salsa and/or sour cream.

# SUNNY SIDE UP BREAKFAST PIZZAS

SERVES 4.

1 lb (500 g) pizza dough
    (see page 230), or a pre-
    made crust
½ to ¾ cup (125 to 185 mL)
    tomato or pizza sauce
1 cup (250 mL) cooked black or
    white beans, or half a 19 oz
    (540 mL) can, rinsed
    and drained

2 cups (500 mL) shredded
    mozzarella or other cheese
Any toppings you like, such as
    mushrooms, finely chopped
    purple onions, roasted
    peppers, thinly sliced
    prosciutto, chopped jarred
    artichokes or olives, and/
    or thawed frozen spinach

with the excess moisture
    squeezed out
1 to 4 large eggs
Basil leaves for garnish
    (optional)

AN EGG CRACKED ON top of your pizza before sliding it into the oven will bake to any degree of doneness you like; try leaving it runny, so that the yolk oozes out when you slice it. Cheese options aren't limited to mozzarella; try shredded Gouda, white cheddar, Edam, or fontina; grated Parmesan; sliced bocconcini; crumbled feta; or a smear of ricotta.

For individual pizzas, divide the dough into 4 pieces and roll each out on a lightly floured surface. To make one big pizza, roll it into an oblong oval, leaving it slightly thicker around the edge to contain the runny egg.

Preheat the oven to 450°F.

Transfer the dough to a heavy baking sheet that has been sprinkled with flour or cornmeal, and spread with tomato sauce; scatter with beans and top with cheese and any toppings you like. Crack an egg into the middle of each individual pizza, or one to four eggs on top of a large oblong pizza. Bake for 15 to 20 minutes, until the crust is golden, the cheese is melted, the egg white is set, and the yolk is done to your liking. Garnish with basil leaves.

# HUEVOS RANCHEROS
## SERVES 1.

**PER PERSON**
**YOU WILL NEED:**
Oil or butter, for cooking
½ to 1 flour or corn tortilla, cut
    in half and then into wide
    strips

Scoop of refried beans,
    either from a can or
    homemade (see page 98)
1 to 2 eggs
Salsa

Large spoonful of guacamole,
    or a few slices of avocado
Sour cream (optional)
Grated Jack cheese (optional)

TRANSLATES TO RANCH Eggs—a big plate of sustaining food for people doing physical work all day. Now a favourite in breakfast joints everywhere, with varied results. We've had too many enormous overstuffed tortillas that turned to mush before we were halfway through. Liberty to the tortilla! Keep it out from under; you won't regret it! Lastly, we need to address the fact that there's a real shortage of hard physical work in a lot of our lives; therefore, scaling back the quantities ain't a bad thing for most of us. If you're a landscape gardener or lumberjack, hats off to you—go ahead and make your Rancheros with three huevos; you deserve it!

Heat a large skillet over medium heat. Put a little oil or butter in the pan and fry the tortilla strips on both sides until browned and crisped; transfer to the side of a dinner-sized plate.

Put the beans on one side of the still-hot pan and cook until heated through, turning and stirring a few times. If you're using cheese, pile it on top of the beans now, leaving them in the pan. Crack an egg or two into the other side of the skillet and cook as desired (or scramble in a bowl first if that's your preference).

Transfer the beans and eggs to the plate with the tortilla strips, and add salsa, guacamole/avocado, sour cream (if using), and more cheese (if using). All can be piled atop the beans and eggs, or spooned to one side. Tuck in.

# ROASTED CHICKPEAS
## & Pecans with Bacon & Maple Syrup
### MAKES ABOUT 1½ CUPS.

1 cup (250 mL) cooked chickpeas, or half a 19 oz (540 mL) can, rinsed and drained

2 to 3 slices bacon, diced
Handful of broken pecans

¼ cup (60 mL) maple syrup
Sea salt to taste

THESE ARE STUPEN-dous as part of a breakfast buffet or an indulgent late-night snack. You can roast the chickpeas ahead of time and then reheat them in the oven before serving if you wish.

Preheat the oven to 325°F.

Spread the chickpeas and bacon over a parchment-lined baking sheet. Bake, stirring once or twice, until the bacon is starting to brown and most of the fat has been rendered, about 30 minutes.

Increase the oven temperature to 400°F and add the pecans. Roast for 5 minutes and add the maple syrup. Toss well and return to the oven for another 3 to 4 minutes. The maple syrup should be thickened and bubbling. Sprinkle lightly with sea salt and allow to cool somewhat before eating.

# SPANISH TORTILLA WITH LENTILS

SERVES 2 AS A HEARTY MEAL, OR YOU CAN CUT IT INTO 6 TO 8 WEDGES FOR A BUFFET OR SIDE DISH.

½ cup (125 mL) dry
   green, brown, or du Puy
   lentils
1 garlic clove, whole
1 bay leaf

Olive oil, for cooking
1 medium red or yellow
   potato, thinly sliced (peeling
   is optional)

1 medium onion,
   thinly sliced
5 large eggs
Salt and pepper

A SPANISH TORTILLA IS a first cousin to the Italian frittata. Simple, but damn fine, and a welcome snack indeed for hiking or kayaking. The preparation time is longer than for many egg dishes, but it can be done ahead—even a day or two ahead—and kept in the refrigerator until close to serving time. You can serve it warm or cold; halfway between the two might even be best. If you're a condiment person, try salsa, ketchup, or chutney; it's also great unadorned.

In a medium saucepan, cook the lentils in 2 cups of water with the bay leaf and whole clove of garlic until soft but not mushy, about 30 to 40 minutes, adding more water if needed. Drain and discard the bay leaf and garlic.

Heat a splash of olive oil in a medium skillet (about 8 inches across the base) over low-moderate heat. Pat the potato slices dry with a clean tea towel or paper towel. Add the onion and potato to the hot pan, seasoning well with salt (about ¼ tsp) and black pepper to taste. Keep the heat fairly low: you want everything to cook before it becomes too brown. Add more olive oil as needed.

When the potatoes are nearly fork-tender (about 20 minutes), add the cooked lentils with another drizzle of olive oil, and place a lid or piece of tin foil over the pan for 5 minutes, stirring once or twice. When the potatoes are tender and the lentils are heated through, taste for seasoning, add a little more oil if required, and turn the heat up to give everything a little colour, another 3 to 5 minutes.

CONTINUED . . .

CONTINUED . . . Meanwhile, break the eggs into a large bowl and season lightly with salt and pepper. Empty the potato mixture into the egg bowl and toss everything well to coat. Give the skillet a quick wash if there are any bits stuck on; if not, just return it to the heat. Add a splash of olive oil to the pan, bring it back to moderate heat, and tip in the egg mixture. Cook on low-moderate heat until the egg is barely set in the centre of the pan, 15 to 20 minutes.

Slide a large plate over the pan and carefully invert the tortilla onto the plate. Slide the tortilla back into the pan (now upside down), just to finish cooking the egg through, another 3 minutes. Remove the pan from the heat and let the tortilla rest a bit before sliding it onto a serving plate.

Beans for Breakfast

# GRANOLA

MAKES 8 TO 10 CUPS.

4 cups (1 L) old-fashioned oats
1 cup (250 mL) barley flakes
¼ cup (60 mL) ground flaxseed
2 cups (500 mL) almonds or
    pecans (or a mix), coarsely
    chopped if you wish
1 cup (250 mL) hulled raw
    sunflower seeds (not salted)

2 cups (500 mL) Candied
    Lentil Meal (page 260)
2 tsp (10 mL) ground cinnamon
¼ tsp (1 mL) nutmeg, preferably
    freshly grated
½ cup (125 mL) honey
2 Tbsp (30 mL) concentrated
    orange or apple juice

2 Tbsp (30 mL) canola oil
½ tsp (2.5 mL) salt
1 cup (250 mL) dried fruit of
    your choice (raisins, cherries,
    cranberries, chopped
    apricots, etc.) (optional)

HOMEMADE GRANOLA really puts store-bought stuff to shame, and the candied lentils make it even more nutritious. Try changing things from batch to batch so you don't tire of the flavours: substitute hazelnuts for the pecans, add sesame seeds or dried coconut, change the barley flakes to millet or rye, and mix up the spices you use.

Preheat the oven to 275°F, and place racks in the upper and lower thirds.

Combine the oats, barley, flaxseed, nuts, seeds, lentils, and spices in a large bowl and toss well. In a small saucepan, melt the honey, concentrated juice, oil, and salt over medium heat, stirring until well combined (no need to boil; you just want the honey very liquid). Drizzle the honey mixture over the dry ingredients and toss until well combined.

Spread the mixture over 2 large rimmed baking sheets and bake for 35 to 45 minutes, stirring once or twice. The granola should be lightly toasted and nearly crisp—it will continue to crisp up as it cools. Cool completely, stir in the dried fruit if you're using it, and store in an airtight container.

# Appies & Snacks

# HUMMUS FIVE WAYS
## MAKES ABOUT 2½ CUPS.

2 cups (500 mL) rinsed and
drained canned chickpeas
(19 oz/540 mL can)
1 large garlic clove, peeled
¼ cup (60 mL) thick plain
yogurt (optional)

Juice of 1 lemon (2 to
3 Tbsp/30 to 45 mL,
or to taste)
2 Tbsp (30 mL) tahini (sesame
seed paste)

½ to 1 tsp (2.5 to 5 mL) ground
cumin (optional)
¼ tsp (1 mL) salt, or to taste
2 to 4 Tbsp (30 to 60 mL)
olive oil

ALL THE MEASURE-
ments here are approxi-
mate—add more or less of
any ingredient to suit your
taste. If you don't have
tahini, use peanut but-
ter. If you love the sesame
flavour of tahini, boost it
with a drizzle of sesame
oil—whether or not you're
using tahini. Flavour your
hummus with anything you
think would work well: try
whizzing in curry powder or
paste, roasted vegetables
or garlic, sun-dried
tomatoes, a chipotle chile,
fresh jalapeño pepper, or
a spoonful of horseradish.

Put everything but the olive oil into the bowl of a food
processor and purée, pouring the olive oil in through
the feed tube as it blends, until smooth. Taste and adjust
seasoning (salt, lemon juice, cumin) as needed. If it's too
thick, add more olive oil, yogurt, or water.

Serve immediately or refrigerate for up to 4 days before
serving.

**VARIATIONS:**

LEMONY PARSLEY
HUMMUS: Add a handful
of chopped fresh parsley
(leave the stems out) and
some extra lemon juice,
or grate some of the zest
and add it, too.

ROASTED BEET
HUMMUS: Wrap 2 medium
beets in tin foil and roast
at 425°F for an hour, or
until tender. Cool, peel,
and slice into chunks; add
to the hummus mixture
as you purée it.

GREEN PEA OR
EDAMAME HUMMUS:
Add a cup of thawed frozen
green peas or steamed
edamame or broad beans.

OLIVE & FETA HUMMUS:
Add a small handful of
pitted olives and a small
chunk of feta, crumbled;
pulse them in at the
end so that they stay
slightly chunky.

# SAMOSAS

MAKES 2½ TO 3 DOZEN SAMOSAS.

**FILLING:**

¼ cup (60 mL) dry red lentils
Canola or olive oil, for cooking
1 onion, finely chopped
2 garlic cloves, crushed
1 Tbsp (15 mL) grated
    fresh ginger
1 tsp (5 mL) curry powder
1 tsp (5 mL) chili powder
½ tsp (2.5 mL) ground cumin

3 cups (750 mL) frozen hash
    browns, thawed
½ cup (125 mL) frozen peas,
    thawed
1 Tbsp (15 mL) lemon juice
1 tsp (5 mL) salt
1 to 2 Tbsp (15 to 30 mL)
    chopped fresh cilantro
    (optional)
1 tsp (5 mL) garam masala

2 Tbsp (30 mL) butter,
    melted
2 Tbsp (30 mL) canola
    or olive oil

1 package (1 lb/500 g) phyllo
    pastry, thawed (you'll need
    about 20 sheets)

WE LIKE TO USE phyllo pastry to wrap up spoonfuls of spiced samosa filling—it's a little more delicate (just like us!) and often easier to find. (If you want to use real samosa wrappers, you can find them fresh or frozen in some well-stocked or ethnic grocery stores. Fry the finished samosas in about an inch of canola oil until golden.)

In a small saucepan, cover the lentils with water; bring to a boil and cook for 15 minutes, until tender. Drain and set aside.

In a large pan, heat a drizzle of oil over medium heat and sauté the onion for about 5 minutes, until soft. Add the garlic, ginger, curry powder, chili powder, and cumin; cook for a minute, then add the hash browns, peas, cooked lentils, lemon juice, and salt. Cook, stirring, for a few minutes, then remove from the heat. Stir in the cilantro (if using) and garam masala. Set aside to cool.

Preheat the oven to 375°F.

To assemble the samosas, stir together the butter and oil in a small dish. Take 2 sheets of phyllo, keeping them stacked together, and place them on a clean work surface; cover the rest with a tea towel so they don't dry out. Brush the phyllo very lightly with the butter-oil mixture.

Cut the stacked sheets in half lengthwise and then cut each half again lengthwise so you have 4 long strips. Place a

spoonful of filling at one end of each strip and fold the corner over diagonally, covering the filling. Continue folding the strip as if you were folding a flag, maintaining the triangle shape.

Repeat with the remaining phyllo (2 sheets at a time) and filling, placing the finished packets seam side down on a baking sheet. (They can be prepared up to this point and frozen in a single layer, then transferred to a plastic bag. Bake them from frozen.) If there is any butter and oil left, use it to brush the tops of the triangles.

Bake for 20 to 25 minutes, until golden. (You may need to add an extra 5 minutes if baking them from frozen.) Serve warm, with mango chutney.

**VARIATION:**

CHICKPEA SAMOSAS: Roughly mash a 19 oz (540 mL) can of rinsed and drained chickpeas with 1 cup (250 mL) cooked quinoa, rice, couscous, or barley; ¼ cup (60 mL) chopped golden raisins; 1 Tbsp (15 mL) grated fresh ginger; 2 crushed garlic cloves; 1 tsp (5 mL) curry powder or paste; 1 tsp (5 mL) ground cumin; and ½ tsp (2.5 mL) salt. Use in place of the filling above.

*Spilling the Beans*

# CURRIED DAL DIP

## SERVES 6 TO 8.

1 cup (250 mL) dry red lentils
Canola oil, for cooking
1 small onion, chopped
2 garlic cloves, crushed
2 tsp (10 mL) curry paste or
    powder

½ cup (125 mL) tomato sauce
    or half a can 156 mL (5.5 oz)
    of tomato paste
1 Tbsp (15 mL) chili powder
1 tsp (5 mL) brown sugar
½ tsp (2.5 mL) salt, or to taste

½ cup (125 mL) plain yogurt,
    half-and-half, evaporated
    milk, or coconut milk
½ tsp (2.5 mL) garam masala
    (optional)
Handful of fresh cilantro,
    chopped (optional)

MADE WITH LENTILS, this dip is reminiscent of chickpea-based hummus. Its flavour improves with time, so you can mix it up a few days ahead and serve it with pita chips and veg whenever you're ready for it. It also makes a great lunch, spread in a pita half stuffed with crunchy vegetables. If you love the flavour of coconut but not the saturated fat in coconut milk, add a teaspoon of coconut extract.

In a medium pot, cover the lentils with water, bring to a boil, and cook for 20 minutes, until very soft. Drain and set aside.

Meanwhile, heat a drizzle of oil in a skillet set over medium-high heat and sauté the onion until golden. Add the garlic and curry paste and cook for another minute. Add the tomato sauce, chili powder, sugar, salt, and cooked lentils and cook for another 5 minutes. Add the yogurt or cream and cook until well blended and thick.

Remove from the heat and stir in the garam masala (if using). Serve immediately or cool and refrigerate until you need it. It can be served warm, at room temperature, or cold, and sprinkled with cilantro if you like.

# EDAMAME OR BROAD BEAN
## *& Walnut Dip*
MAKES ABOUT 2½ CUPS.

1 cup (250 mL) fresh or frozen (thawed) shelled edamame (soybeans) or broad beans

1 cup (250 mL) walnut halves or pieces, toasted

½ to 1 cup (125 to 250 mL) fresh parsley (stems removed)

½ cup (125 mL) plain yogurt or sour cream

2 Tbsp (30 mL) olive or canola oil

1 garlic clove, crushed

¼ tsp (1 mL) salt

NO, THIS DIP AIN'T pretty. But it's damn tasty, and that's all that really matters. Besides, with all those beans, nuts, and greens, it's very good for you, especially for a dip, which generally consists primarily of sour cream, mayo, and/or cream cheese. Serve with toasted pita chips. Its flavour improves after a day or two to hang out in the refrigerator.

Steam the edamame or broad beans in a small pot with about ½ inch of water for 5 minutes. Drain and set aside to cool.

In the bowl of a food processor, pulse the steamed edamame with the remaining ingredients until well blended and as smooth or chunky as you like. Serve immediately or cover and refrigerate for a day or two.

# SPICED ROASTED CHICKPEAS
## *with Walnuts*
### MAKES 2 TO 3 CUPS.

19 oz (540 mL) can chickpeas, rinsed and well drained

¼ cup (60 mL) canola or olive oil

1 tsp (5 mL) ground cumin

1 tsp (5 mL) paprika

1 tsp (5 mL) coarse salt, or to taste

½ tsp (2.5 mL) freshly ground black pepper, or to taste

1 to 2 cups (250 to 500 mL) walnut halves

WE ARE BOTH FANS OF salty, snacky things we can eat with our fingers. (Is there anyone out there who isn't?) Roasted and salted, chickpeas easily fall into this category, and pair well with toasted nuts, even right in the same bowl. We tossed these with spices first; experiment with different spice blends—anything you'd typically use to make spiced nuts would work well here.

If there are any left over, they're brilliant on a salad.

Preheat the oven to 400°F.

In a medium bowl, combine the chickpeas, oil, cumin, paprika, salt, and pepper. Spread out in a single layer on a rimmed baking sheet and roast for about 20 minutes, stirring once or twice, until golden.

Add the walnuts, toss the mixture around again, and roast for another 10 minutes, until the walnuts and chickpeas are golden. Season with extra salt, if needed, and serve immediately.

# ANTIPASTO

MAKES ABOUT 16 CUPS.

1 cup (250 mL) olive or canola oil, or some of each

1 small head cauliflower, separated into small florets

1 large or 2 medium purple onions, peeled and chopped

Two 12 oz (355 mL) cans or jars pitted black olives, drained and sliced

Two 12 oz (355 mL) cans or jars manzanilla olives, drained and sliced

2 red or yellow bell peppers, seeded and finely chopped

½ lb (250 g) cooked small cocktail shrimp, or chopped larger shrimp

Two 6 oz (170 g) cans tuna in water, drained

2 cups (500 mL) cooked white beans, or a 19 oz (540 mL) can, rinsed and drained

3½ cups (875 mL) ketchup

1 cup (250 mL) white vinegar

Two 10 oz (284 mL) cans mushroom slices or pieces, drained

ANTIPASTO ISN'T difficult to make, but it does require a lot of chopping. Don't be tempted to use a food processor—the texture just won't be the same. This recipe will make a lot, but it freezes well and can be preserved in jars, so you'll be set up for party snacks and gifts for food lovers for a good long while.

In a very large pot, combine the oil, cauliflower, onions, and olives and bring it all to a simmer over medium-high heat. Cook, stirring often, for 5 minutes. (Just make sure it's cooking to the point where any juices you see are bubbling.)

Add the remaining ingredients and heat just until the mixture comes to a boil. Remove from the heat, let the antipasto cool completely, and then transfer to containers to store in the refrigerator for up to a week, or freeze for up to 6 months.

# CHEESY BLACK BEAN DIP

### SERVES 6 TO 8.

2 cups (500 mL) rinsed
  and drained canned
  black or red kidney beans
  (19 oz/540 mL can)
Canola or olive oil, for cooking
1 small onion or 2 to 3 green
  onions, chopped

2 garlic cloves, crushed
1 Roma (or plum) tomato,
  finely chopped
½ cup (125 mL) salsa
1 Tbsp (15 mL) chili powder
½ tsp (2.5 mL) ground cumin

1 cup (250 mL) shredded
  old cheddar or Monterey
  Jack cheese
1 Tbsp (15 mL) lime juice
¼ cup (60 mL) chopped fresh
  cilantro (optional)

IN OUR EXPERIENCE, kids (and grown-ups) can almost always be coerced to eat beans if they're served in a warm, cheesy dip meant to be scooped up with tortilla chips. Canned beans work best for dips, as they tend to be more mushable—if you start with dry beans, cook them a little longer to soften them up. If you want to up the heat a bit, add a chopped jalapeño pepper or can of green chilies along with the salsa (recipe originally appeared in *Grazing*).

Mash the drained black beans with a fork right in the can (or a bowl) until chunky; don't squish them all—it's nice to keep some texture.

In a large skillet, heat a drizzle of oil over medium-high heat. Sauté the onion and garlic for a few minutes, until soft. Add the beans, tomato, salsa, chili powder, and cumin and cook until heated through. Stir in the cheese and lime juice and cook until the cheese begins to melt. Stir in the cilantro, if you're using it.

Serve warm, with tortilla chips.

# HOISIN BLACK BEAN
## *Lettuce Wraps*
### MAKES ABOUT 16 WRAPS.

1 lb (500 g) pork tenderloin, skinless, boneless chicken thighs, or raw peeled shrimp

Canola, olive, or sesame oil, for cooking

2 garlic cloves, crushed

1 Tbsp (15 mL) grated fresh ginger

2 cups (500 mL) fresh mushrooms, chopped (any kind or combination)

1 small red pepper, seeded and finely chopped

1 cup (250 mL) cooked black beans, or half a 19 oz (540 mL) can, rinsed and drained

¼ cup (60 mL) bottled hoisin sauce, or to taste

Half an 8 oz (227 mL) can water chestnuts, drained and chopped (optional)

Salt and pepper to taste

2 green onions, chopped

2 romaine lettuce hearts (the outer leaves tend to be too large), or a head of butter or leaf lettuce

YOU MAY RECOGNIZE lettuce wraps from restaurant menus. They're easy to make and stylish to serve on a platter—present a bowl of filling with lettuce leaves on the side and have everyone scoop filling onto a leaf, wrap, and eat. It's great for parties, and makes a perfect eat-with-your-fingers meal—real food to munch on when you're planted on the couch.

Cut the pork or chicken into small strips or ½-inch pieces, or if you're using shrimp, cut them in half lengthwise. Heat a drizzle of oil in a large skillet set over medium-high heat and sauté the pork, chicken, or shrimp for a few minutes, until opaque. If you're using shrimp, remove it from the pan and set aside. Add the garlic and ginger and cook for another minute. Add the mushrooms and red pepper and cook until they release their moisture, then start to brown. Add the black beans and hoisin sauce and toss to coat and heat through; add the water chestnuts (if using), salt and pepper, and green onions. If you used shrimp, stir it back in. Remove from the heat and transfer to a bowl.

Wash the lettuce well, spin it dry, and separate into leaves. Arrange it on a platter with the bowl of hoisin filling. To eat, pile some of the mixture onto a lettuce leaf, wrap it up, and eat it like a burrito.

# MARINATED ROASTED EGGPLANT,

## *Pepper & Mushrooms with Lentils*

### MAKES 3 TO 4 CUPS.

½ cup (125 mL) dry green
   or brown lentils
2 garlic cloves, left whole
1 medium eggplant
1 red bell pepper
2 to 3 portobello mushrooms
   (about 4 oz/125 g total),
   or other mushrooms

**DRESSING:**
2 pinches of fennel seed
¼ tsp (1 mL) dried oregano
¼ tsp (1 mL) dried rosemary
¼ tsp (1 mL) salt
¼ tsp (1 mL) garlic powder
Freshly ground black pepper
   to taste

Dried red chili flakes
   to taste (optional)
⅓ cup (80 mL) olive oil
1½ Tbsp (22.5 mL) red wine
   vinegar

THIS DISH IS VERY much like the marinated mix of peppers and mushrooms available at Italian markets, but with a lot less oil. Spoon it onto crostini or a rustic ciabatta, or use as a condiment on sandwiches or burgers. If you have a barbecue and some fine weather, grilling the vegetables will add even more flavour.

In a medium saucepan, cook the lentils in 2 cups of water with the 2 whole garlic cloves until soft but not mushy, about 30 to 40 minutes. If the pan is in danger of drying out before the lentils are cooked, add more water as needed, about ½ cup at a time. Discard the garlic when done.

While the lentils are cooking, peel the eggplant and cut lengthwise into ¼-inch-thick slices. Lightly salt both sides of each slice, then place them in a colander set in the sink. Let the eggplant sit for 30 or more minutes while the salt draws out the moisture.

TO ROAST AND PEEL THE PEPPER: Place the whole pepper under the broiler for about 5 to 8 minutes, turning frequently, until the skin is blackened and blistered in places and the flesh is starting to soften. Place the pepper in a medium bowl and cover for at least 10 minutes. When it's cool enough to handle, remove the skin (it should slide off easily), and pull out the core and seeds. Don't rinse it, though—you'll wash away the flavour! Cut into thin strips

CONTINUED . . .

CONTINUED ... (about ¼ inch wide by 1½ inches long) and set aside in a medium bowl.

Preheat the oven to 425°F.

Gently wipe any dirt off the mushrooms and, if using portobellos, remove the stems and scrape the gills out with a spoon. Cut the cleaned mushrooms into ¼-inch-thick slices and place on a large rimmed baking sheet. Retrieve the slices of eggplant and pat dry with a tea towel. Slice the pieces into strips about 1 inch by 2 inches and add to the mushrooms.

Crush the fennel, oregano, and rosemary with a mortar and pestle, transfer to a small bowl or jar, and add the salt, garlic powder, black pepper, dried red chili flakes (if using), and olive oil. Pour half of this mixture over the eggplant and mushrooms and toss well. Roast for 25 to 30 minutes, stirring occasionally, until the vegetables are golden and cooked through. Loosen the roasted vegetables from the baking sheet and allow to cool slightly.

Add the red wine vinegar to the remaining oil and herbs, and add to the peppers along with the lentils, roasted eggplant, and mushrooms. If there are any juices lingering on the baking sheet, scrape them in, too. Toss well, and refrigerate for at least a couple of hours—preferably overnight. The vinegar will start off quite strong but will mellow out with a little time. If you prefer the mix a little more oily, by all means give it a good drizzle.

# WHITE BEAN,
## *Tomato & Olive Bruschetta*
MAKES ABOUT 2 DOZEN CROSTINI.

**CROSTINI:**

Half a thin baguette,
cut into ½-inch (1 cm) slices
on a slight diagonal

¼ cup (60 mL) olive or canola
oil, plus extra if you need it

1 garlic clove, peeled and
crushed

2 cups (500 mL) cooked white
beans, or a 19 oz (540 mL)
can, rinsed and drained

3 ripe plum tomatoes, seeded
and chopped

¼ to ½ cup (60 to 125 mL)
kalamata olives, pitted
and chopped

¼ cup (60 mL) chopped fresh
basil or flat-leaf parsley

1 Tbsp (15 mL) balsamic
vinegar

1 garlic clove, crushed

Salt and pepper to taste

½ cup (125 mL) or about
4 oz (125 g) soft fresh
goat cheese or Parmesan
cheese (optional)

A TASTY JUMBLE OF white beans, tomato, garlic, olives, and basil is simple to serve in a bowl along with crostini (toasted baguette). To extract the pits from the olives, smash the olives on a board with the flat side of your knife blade—the pits will pop right out.

Preheat the oven to 400°F.

Place the baguette slices on a rimmed baking sheet. Fill a small dish with the oil and put the garlic clove in it; brush the baguette slices lightly with the oil and bake for 5 to 10 minutes, until pale golden. Flip them over, brush the other sides, and bake for another 3 to 4 minutes.

In a medium bowl, lightly crush the beans with a fork, keeping them chunky. Stir the oil left from the crostini (if you used it all, add a couple more tablespoons) along with the tomatoes, olives, basil, vinegar, garlic, and salt and pepper. Stir until well blended. (The mixture can be made ahead to this point and refrigerated overnight.)

If you're using goat cheese, spread it on the toasts and spoon the bean mixture on top. If you're using Parmesan instead, spoon the bean mixture onto the toasts and sprinkle the grated cheese on top—we like to shave off big curls from a block of Parmesan using a vegetable peeler.

# SAVOURY HAND PIES
## *with Sun-Dried Tomatoes, Lentils, Olives & Feta*
### MAKES 12 TO 15 PIES.

**PASTRY:**

2½ cups (625 mL) all-purpose
    flour
½ tsp (2.5 mL) sugar
½ tsp (2.5 mL) salt
¾ cup (185 mL) cold butter
5 Tbsp (75 mL) ice water, plus
    a little more if required

**FILLING:**

¼ cup (60 mL) dry green lentils
    (or ¾ cup/185 mL canned,
    rinsed and drained)
¼ cup (60 mL) kalamata olives
    (about 8 to 10)
¼ cup (60 mL) sun-dried toma-
    toes packed in oil, drained
    and finely chopped

¼ cup (60 mL) feta cheese,
    finely chopped
1 Tbsp (15 mL) finely chopped
    fresh parsley
Freshly ground black pepper
    to taste
1 egg, lightly beaten with 1 tsp
    (5 mL) water to make a wash
    (optional)

EVER PUT LITTLE PIES out among a group of people, and seen them disappear as if magic were involved? We have, with these pies and their wonderfully summery Mediterranean filling. The pastry works well with all-purpose flour or a mix of all-purpose and whole wheat pastry flours. Don't let pie dough intimidate you—just patch the cracks together as you're roll-ing it out and it will be fine. Remember—you're the boss of the pastry.

TO MAKE THE PASTRY: In a large bowl, stir together the flour, sugar, and salt. Cut the butter into cubes, grate on the coarse side of a box grater, or shave curls with a vegetable peeler directly into the bowl. Using a pastry blender or a fork, work the butter into the flour until it resembles coarse meal. Add the ice water tablespoon by tablespoon and toss until the mixture clumps together, trying to use as little additional water as possible. Form into 2 balls, and then flatten into discs, smoothing and squishing it together where it cracks. (Handle it as little as possible—the warmth from your hands could melt the butter, and overworking can make pastry tough.) Wrap each disc with plastic wrap and chill for at least an hour, or overnight. (It can also be frozen for up to 4 months.) Let the dough come to room temperature again before rolling it out.

TO MAKE THE FILLING: Cook the lentils in 1¼ cups water, with a lid on, until tender, 30 to 40 minutes. Drain and set aside to cool.

Preheat the oven to 400°F.

Place the olives on a cutting board and crush them one by one with the flat side of a large knife. Remove the pits and finely chop the olives. In a medium bowl, stir together the cooled lentils, olives, sun-dried tomatoes, feta, parsley, and pepper.

On a lightly floured board, roll out the pastry to less than a ⅛-inch thickness. Cut out 4-inch rounds, re-rolling scraps once. Spoon 1 Tbsp of filling onto each round, then fold into a half-moon shape, crimping the edges shut with a fork. Place the pies on a baking sheet 1 inch apart and brush the top of each with the egg wash (if using). Cut 3 slits in the top of each pie with a sharp knife to let steam escape, and bake until the pastry is crisp and golden, 15 to 20 minutes. Cool on a wire rack.

# SPINACH & ARTICHOKE DIP
## with White Beans
### SERVES 6 TO 8.

8 oz (250 g) package light
cream cheese, softened
2 Tbsp (30 mL) mayonnaise
1 cup (250 mL) rinsed and
drained canned white beans
(half a 19 oz/540 mL can)
2 garlic cloves, crushed

6 oz (170 mL) jar marinated
artichoke hearts, drained
and coarsely chopped
10 oz (300 g) package
frozen chopped spinach,
thawed and excess liquid
squeezed out

¼ cup (60 mL) grated
Parmesan cheese
¼ cup (60 mL) shredded
mozzarella cheese, divided
Few dashes hot sauce
(optional)
Salt and freshly ground black
pepper to taste

WE'VE BEEN BURNED ordering this in pubs too many times: what seems like a good idea when you're hungry becomes a heavy, greasy shame. But it doesn't need to be like that—this dip will treat you right, and you'll still respect each other in the morning. You can make it for a crowd or split it in two and bake one for tonight and freeze one for later.

Preheat the oven to 350°F.

Place the cream cheese, mayonnaise, beans, and garlic in the bowl of a food processor and pulse until smooth. Scrape into a bowl and stir in the chopped artichoke hearts, drained spinach, Parmesan, half the mozzarella cheese, and hot sauce (if using). Taste and add pepper and salt, if it needs it (the artichokes and cheese may be salty enough).

Transfer to a shallow baking dish that has been sprayed with non-stick cooking spray and smooth the top. Cover loosely with tin foil (taking care that the tin foil isn't resting on the dip) and bake for 30 minutes, until warmed through. Remove the tin foil, sprinkle with the remaining cheese, and bake another 10 to 15 minutes, until the cheese is melted and the edges are bubbly. Serve warm with pita, ciabatta, crackers, or tortilla chips.

# VIETNAMESE RICE PAPER ROLLS

MAKES ABOUT 1 CUP OF SAUCE AND 8 ROLLS.

**FILLING (QUANTITIES ARE REALLY UP TO YOU):**

Large handful of thin rice vermicelli noodles

1 Tbsp (15 mL) rice vinegar

1 tsp (5 mL) sugar

1 small carrot

5-inch chunk of cucumber

½ red, yellow, or orange bell pepper

Handful or two of salad greens

1 cup (250 mL) mixed sprouted beans (half an 8 oz/225 g container), steamed or blanched briefly if you like

Chopped fresh cilantro (optional)

8 rice paper wrappers, 8 inches in diameter (or more of the smaller ones if you prefer)

**PEANUT SAUCE:**

¼ cup (60 mL) peanut butter

2 Tbsp (30 mL) chicken stock, coconut milk, or water

3 Tbsp (45 mL) soy sauce

2 Tbsp (30 mL) brown sugar or honey

2 Tbsp (30 mL) rice vinegar or lime juice

1 garlic clove, crushed

1 tsp (5 mL) grated fresh ginger

¼ to ½ tsp (1 to 2.5 mL) curry paste (optional)

YOU CAN CHANGE these up endlessly to suit your tastes. Rice paper rolls often include cooked shrimp, shredded roast meats (try leftover chicken or pork), fresh mango, and nearly any crunchy vegetable you can think of—asparagus, jicama, and pea pods work especially well. Rice paper rolls make a fantastic packed lunch—the other kids will be jealous! Briefly steaming or blanching the sprouted beans will brighten them and get rid of any chalky texture.

Place the rice noodles in a bowl and cover with boiling water. Let stand until just softened, about 2 to 3 minutes; drain and toss with the vinegar and sugar. Use scissors to cut the tangle of noodles in a few places, just so you're able to separate the mass into small portions.

Using a vegetable peeler, shave the carrot into thin strips, or grate it with the coarse side of a box grater. Peel the cucumber if it needs it, cut it in half lengthwise, and slice into ¼-inch-thick slices. If you like, cut the pieces crosswise in half. Cut the red pepper into sticks of similar size and slice the greens into coarse shreds.

On a dinner plate or cutting board, assemble 8 small, slightly oblong stacks of filling ingredients (except sprouted beans and cilantro), a little of each making up one stack. Fold a clean, dry tea towel in half and place it on your work surface. Fill a shallow dish (a pie plate is perfect) with hot tap water, and, working one at a time, slide a rice paper wrapper into the hot water for about 5 to 10 seconds. You'll want it to be starting to soften, but only just. Pull the wrapper out of the water and place on the tea towel (and if it's excessively wet, pat the surface dry with the edge of the towel). Place a stack of filling in the centre, and add a spoonful of sprouted beans and a sprinkling of cilantro (if using). Fold one side of the wrapper over a long side of the filling, fold over both ends, then roll up as tightly as you can without tearing the wrapper. Serve the rice paper rolls with peanut sauce for dipping.

TO MAKE THE PEANUT SAUCE: combine all the ingredients in a blender or jar and whiz or shake until smooth. Refrigerate until you're ready to serve it.

**HINTS IF YOU'RE NEW TO RICE PAPER ROLLING:**

» It's easier if you use less filling for the first few you make.
» You need to work quickly after the wrapper has been moistened, because they get quite fragile. If a roll splits open, you can always encase the whole thing in a second wrapper.
» It's a good idea to have extra wrappers on hand, as most of us tear a few as we're working.
» While you're preparing these, stack the finished rolls so they don't touch one another, as they can stick together, leading to torn wrappers. They get a little more sturdy when they've had a chance to sit for a bit.

Beany, Grainy Salads

# CURRIED QUINOA SALAD
## *with Black Beans & Mango*
SERVES 4 TO 6 (OR 2, IF IT'S US).

1 cup (250 mL) quinoa

1 to 2 ripe mangoes, peeled and chopped

½ red or yellow bell pepper, chopped

¼ English cucumber, chopped

2 to 3 green onions or a chunk of purple onion, chopped

2 cups (500 mL) packed baby spinach, torn or sliced (optional)

Handful of torn fresh cilantro (optional)

1 cup (250 mL) cooked black beans, or half a 19 oz (540 mL) can, rinsed and drained

**DRESSING:**

¼ cup (60 mL) canola oil

2 to 4 Tbsp (30 to 60 mL) white wine or white balsamic vinegar

1 tsp (5 mL) honey or brown sugar

1 tsp (5 mL) curry powder or mild paste

¼ tsp (1 mL) ground cumin

THIS IS ONE OF OUR hands-down all-time-favourite ways to reach our beans and grains quota. Quinoa (pronounced KEEN-wah), actually a seed related to kale but treated as a grain, makes a great light, high-protein base for a portable salad. The earthy black beans and sweetness of the mango go well with the curried dressing, but it can of course be customized however you like. It's just a big ol' bowl of yum.

Rinse the quinoa well under cool water in a fine sieve, then cook in a pot of boiling salted water over medium heat until tender but still firm to the bite, stirring occasionally, about 15 minutes. (Cook it just like you'd cook pasta.) Drain well, return it to the pot, put the lid back on and let it steam—this will produce fluffy quinoa—until cooled.

TO MAKE THE DRESSING: combine the oil, vinegar, honey, curry, and cumin in a jar or small bowl and shake or whisk to blend.

In a large bowl, combine the quinoa, mangoes, vegetables, and beans; drizzle with dressing and toss until well coated. Chill until ready to serve, or eat immediately if you prefer.

# BARLEY & WHEAT BERRY SALAD
## *with Chickpeas & Feta*
SERVES 6 TO 8.

½ cup (125 mL) wheat berries

½ cup (125 mL) pearl or
pot barley

¼ to ½ cup (60 to 125 mL)
chopped dates or dried figs

2 cups (500 mL) cooked
chickpeas, or a 19 oz

(540 mL) can, rinsed
and drained

½ cup (125 mL) crumbled
feta cheese

2 celery stalks, chopped

½ cup (125 mL) chopped
walnuts, toasted

¼ cup (60 mL) olive
or canola oil

3 Tbsp (45 mL) red wine
vinegar or lemon juice

Salt and freshly ground black
pepper to taste

NUTTY WHEAT BERRIES are well worth seeking out; they make a great foundation for a salad—similar to barley but mahogany-coloured and smooth. They do need a pre-soak, but you're used to doing that with the beans, aren't you? If they aren't pre-soaked, they'll just need some extra time in the boiling pot.

In a medium saucepan, cover the wheat berries with a few inches of water; bring to a boil. Remove from the heat and let stand for an hour. (Alternatively, soak them in water overnight.)

Pour off most of the water from the wheat berries, add the barley to the pot, and cover with water by a few inches; bring to a boil and cook for 45 minutes, until both the barley and wheat berries are tender. Drain and rinse under cold water to stop them from cooking; drain well and transfer to a bowl. Stir in the dates or figs and let cool completely.

Add the chickpeas, feta, celery, and walnuts to the cooled grains. Drizzle with the oil and vinegar and sprinkle with salt and pepper; toss to combine. Serve immediately or refrigerate until needed.

# LENTIL & BARLEY SALAD
## with Tomatoes, Spinach & Feta
### SERVES 4 TO 6.

½ cup (125 mL) dry
green lentils

½ cup (125 mL) pot or
pearl barley

1 garlic clove, peeled
(optional)

1 tomato, chopped,
or a handful of grape
tomatoes, halved

1 packed cup (250 mL) fresh
spinach or flat-leaf parsley,
chopped

½ cup (125 mL) crumbled
feta cheese

¼ small purple onion,
finely chopped

Freshly ground black
pepper

**DRESSING:**

¼ cup (60 mL) olive or
canola oil

¼ cup (60 mL) balsamic
vinegar or lemon juice

1 Tbsp (15 mL) grainy mustard

1 tsp (5 mL) maple syrup
or honey

1 garlic clove, crushed

GREEN LENTILS AND barley cook in the same length of time, so you can boil them together for grainy salads or to add to soup. Cooked, they freeze well—if you want to make a big batch while you're at it, freeze cupfuls of green lentils and barley in freezer bags (without additional liquid) to toss in soup or use as a base for another salad. It's real convenience food from your own private freezer aisle.

Put the lentils, barley, and garlic clove (if using) in a medium pot and add water to cover by a couple inches; bring to a boil and cook for 45 minutes, or until tender. Drain well, discard the garlic clove, and set aside to cool.

In a large bowl, combine the cooled lentils and barley, tomato, spinach, feta, and onion; grind some black pepper overtop.

Shake up the dressing ingredients in a small jar or whisk in a bowl; pour over the salad and toss to coat. Serve immediately, or refrigerate until needed.

# BROWN & WILD RICE & BARLEY SALAD
## *with Chickpeas*
### SERVES 4 AS A MAIN OR 8 AS A SIDE.

⅓ cup (80 mL) brown rice
⅓ cup (80 mL) wild rice
⅓ cup (80 mL) pearl
   or pot barley
2 cups (500 mL) cooked
   chickpeas, or a 19 oz
   (540 mL) can, rinsed
   and drained

⅓ cup (80 mL) golden raisins
1 cup (250 mL) grape tomatoes,
   halved
2 to 3 green onions, chopped
   (optional)
1 small bunch fresh curly or flat-
   leaf parsley, chopped
¼ cup (60 mL) toasted pecans
   or almonds

**DRESSING:**
3 Tbsp (45 mL) red wine
   or balsamic vinegar
3 Tbsp (45 mL) canola
   or olive oil
2 tsp (10 mL) grainy mustard
1 tsp (5 mL) brown sugar
½ tsp (2.5 mL) curry paste
   or powder

GOOD NEWS: BROWN and wild rice and barley all cook for the same length of time, so you can cook them up together if you want to make a grainy salad or pilaf. (Do people even make pilaf anymore? It's fun to say, though. "Pilaf!")

The tomatoes, raisins, green onions, and parsley add a good assortment of flavours and textures, but feel free to ad lib here.

In a large pot of boiling water, cook the brown rice, wild rice, and barley for 40 to 45 minutes, until tender. Drain and run under cool water to stop the grains from cooking. Drain well and transfer to a bowl; add the chickpeas and raisins.

Whisk together all the dressing ingredients (adjusting them to suit your taste) and pour overtop. Chill in the refrigerator until the mixture is completely cool, or for up to a day.

Add the tomatoes, green onions (if using), parsley, and pecans (or save them to sprinkle on top) and serve.

# MARINATED LENTIL COUSCOUS SALAD

SERVES 6 TO 10 (DEPENDING ON WHETHER IT'S A SIDE DISH
OR THE MAIN EVENT).

1 cup (250 mL) dry green
or brown lentils
1 garlic clove, peeled
2 Tbsp (30 mL) white wine
or white balsamic vinegar
1 Tbsp (15 mL) sugar or honey
1 cup (250 mL) couscous
1 ¼ cups (310 mL) boiling water
Salt to taste

2 cups (500 mL) grape or
cherry tomatoes, whole
or halved
½ English cucumber, chopped
2 cups (500 mL) packed
baby spinach leaves, torn or
chopped, or ½ cup (125 mL)
chopped fresh parsley, mint,
or a combination

½ cup (125 mL) crumbled
feta cheese

**DRESSING:**
¼ cup (60 mL) olive or
canola oil
¼ cup (60 mL) white wine
or white balsamic vinegar
1 garlic clove, crushed

THIS IS ANOTHER ONE of those anything-goes salads—couscous and lentils make a delicious base (as do barley and lentils) that's perfect for transporting to parties or picnics, or for lunch at work. The great thing about salads is that you really don't have to use a specific list of ingredients, or adhere to any measurements. If you want a bigger batch, just double the quantity of couscous.

Put the lentils and garlic in a small pot and add 2½ cups of water. Bring to a simmer, cover, and cook for 30 minutes, until tender. Drain and toss with the vinegar and sugar while still warm.

Meanwhile, put the couscous in a large bowl and pour the boiling water overtop; cover with a plate and let sit for 10 minutes, or until all the water is absorbed. Fluff with a fork and stir in the lentils. Put into the refrigerator to chill.

When the couscous-lentil mixture is cool, add the tomatoes, cucumber, spinach, and feta.

Shake the dressing ingredients together in a jar or whisk them in a small bowl and pour over the salad; toss to coat.

# QUINOA, CAULIFLOWER,
## *Chickpea & Feta Sort-of-Slaw*
### SERVES 6.

½ cup (125 mL) quinoa
½ small head cauliflower, roughly chopped
2 to 4 cups (500 mL to 1 L) bagged coleslaw (about half a bag)
1 cup (250 mL) cooked chickpeas or white beans,

or half a 19 oz (540 mL) can, rinsed and drained
1 apple, cored and chopped
½ cup (125 mL) crumbled feta cheese
Freshly ground black pepper to taste

**DRESSING:**
¼ cup (60 mL) olive or canola oil
Juice of 1 lemon
2 Tbsp (30 mL) rice, white wine, or white balsamic vinegar
2 tsp (10 mL) sugar or honey
1 tsp (5 mL) grainy mustard

THIS IS A CRAZY-looking—and delicious—jumble of salad in shades of off-white. We must say, it's mighty refreshing to just hack up a chunk of cauliflower, rather than fiddle with separating all those finicky little florets. Grate the zest of your lemon into the salad, too, if you like things lemony.

Rinse the quinoa well under cool water in a fine sieve, then cook in a pot of boiling salted water over medium heat until tender but still firm to the bite, stirring occasionally, about 15 minutes. (Cook it just like you'd cook pasta.) Drain well, return it to the pot, put the lid back on, and let it steam—this will produce fluffy quinoa—until cooled.

Once cool, transfer the quinoa to a bowl and add the cauliflower, coleslaw, chickpeas, apple, and feta, and sprinkle with pepper.

In a small bowl or jar, whisk or shake together the dressing ingredients. Drizzle the salad with dressing and toss to coat.

Beany, Grainy Salads

# CHARRED CORN, BLACK BEAN
## & Toasted Barley Salad
### SERVES 4 TO 6.

½ cup (125 mL) pearl or
    pot barley
1½ cups (375 mL) chicken
    or vegetable stock or water
Canola or olive oil, for cooking
2 ears fresh corn, husked
    (or 1 cup/250 mL frozen or
    canned kernel corn)
1 cup (250 mL) cooked
    black beans, or half a 19 oz
    (540 mL) can, rinsed
    and drained

½ red or yellow bell pepper,
    seeded and chopped
1 small tomato, diced
1 ripe mango, peeled and diced
¼ purple onion, finely chopped
¼ to ½ cup (60 to 125 mL)
    chopped fresh flat-leaf
    parsley (minus stems)
    or cilantro (optional)

**DRESSING:**
⅓ cup (80 mL) canola
    or olive oil
¼ cup (60 mL) lime juice
1 tsp (5 mL) ground cumin
1 tsp (5 mL) honey
1 garlic clove, crushed

THERE ARE A THOU-sand delicious combinations that involve barley and black beans—this one has a bit of a Mexican slant, so it's great made with cooked, cooled rice as well. Or try quinoa or couscous. Warm it up with a bit of chipotle powder or sauce in the dressing, or turn it into a more substantial meal by topping it with some quickly sautéed shrimp or a piece of grilled chicken.

In a medium saucepan, toast the dry barley over medium-high heat for a few minutes, or until golden and toasty-smelling. Pour in the stock or water, bring to a boil, turn the heat down, cover, and cook for about 40 minutes, until tender. Transfer to a bowl to cool completely.

In a heavy skillet, heat a drizzle of oil over medium-high heat. Scrape the kernels of corn from the cob and sauté for 5 minutes, or until starting to turn golden. Set aside to cool.

In a small bowl or jar, combine all the dressing ingredients and whisk or shake to combine. In a large bowl, toss together the cooled barley, corn, beans, pepper, tomato, mango, onion, and parsley (if using). Drizzle with dressing and toss to coat. Serve immediately or refrigerate for up to a few hours before serving.

# RICE OR ORZO SALAD
## *with Chickpeas, Spinach, Lemon & Feta*
### SERVES 6 TO 8, OR MORE IF IT'S PART OF A BUFFET.

1½ cups (375 mL) long-grain
   rice or orzo
Few handfuls of pre-washed
   baby spinach (about half a
   10 oz/300 g bag)
2 cups (500 mL) cooked
   chickpeas, or a 19 oz

(540 mL) can, rinsed
   and drained
½ small purple onion,
   finely chopped
1 cup (250 mL) crumbled
   feta cheese

Grated zest and juice
   of 1 lemon
¼ cup (60 mL) canola or olive
   oil, or to taste
¼ cup (60 mL) rice vinegar,
   or to taste
Salt and pepper to taste

WE INVENTED THIS lemony salad for a baby shower years ago—it's great when you need to feed a crowd and it keeps really well in the refrigerator, so you can mix up a big batch and be well fed all week if it's all for you. To up the quantity, just boost amounts of each ingredient—it's easy to wing it with this. It's delicious made with rice or orzo (small rice-shaped pasta) or even Israeli couscous (which is larger than the more common kind). Try using brown rice for added fibre and B vitamins.

Cook the rice or orzo according to package directions, drain, and transfer to a large bowl to cool completely.

To slice the spinach, stack a bunch of leaves, roll them up tightly, and thinly slice the whole bunch—this is the fastest way to get through large quantities of spinach. Add the sliced spinach to the cooled rice along with the chickpeas, onion, feta, and lemon zest. Toss everything well.

Squeeze the lemon juice over the salad, drizzle with the oil and rice vinegar, and add salt and pepper. Toss to coat well. Taste and adjust the seasonings if necessary. Serve immediately or refrigerate until you're ready for it.

Beany, Grainy Salads

# CLASSIC THREE-BEAN SALAD

### SERVES 8 TO 10.

14 oz (398 mL) can cut green beans, drained

14 oz (398 mL) can cut yellow wax beans, drained

14 oz (398 mL) can kidney beans, rinsed and drained

19 oz (540 mL) can chickpeas, rinsed and drained

1 red bell pepper, seeded and chopped

2 celery stalks, chopped

1 small purple onion, finely chopped

¼ cup (60 mL) chopped fresh parsley (optional)

½ cup (125 mL) red wine vinegar or white vinegar

⅓ cup (80 mL) sugar or honey

¼ cup (60 mL) canola oil

1 garlic clove, crushed (optional)

Salt and pepper to taste

THE GREAT THING about bean salad, besides the fact that it's crazy easy to make and incredibly good for you, is that it keeps in the refrigerator for ages and its flavour actually improves over time as the beans have a chance to bask in the vinaigrette. Because you need a wide variety of beans, this recipe makes a large batch, but large batches are a Very Good Thing if you like having something prepared in the refrigerator to dip into all week or if you've been asked to bring something that will feed lots of people.

Combine all the beans, vegetables, and parsley (if using) in a large bowl. In a small saucepan, combine the vinegar, sugar, oil, garlic (if using), and salt and pepper. Set it over medium heat and bring the mixture to a simmer. Cook for a few minutes, until the sugar dissolves completely. Set the vinaigrette aside to cool for a few minutes before pouring it over the salad. Toss gently to coat all the beans with dressing.

Cover and refrigerate overnight to allow the beans to marinate, and serve the salad cold.

NOTE:
If you want to use fresh green and yellow beans, trim off the ends and steam them for just a few minutes, until they're tender-crisp, then plunge them into cold water to stop them from cooking further, and drain them well.

# APPLE, SPROUTED BEAN
## *& Crystallized Ginger Salad with Cambozola*

MAKES 4 STARTER SALADS OR 2 MAIN COURSE SALADS.

**DRESSING:**
1 Tbsp (15 mL) canola oil
1 Tbsp (15 mL) olive oil
2 tsp (10 mL) white wine
  vinegar
½ tsp (2.5 mL) honey thinned
  with ½ tsp (2.5 mL) water
1 garlic clove, crushed
Salt and black pepper to taste

**SALAD:**
4 big handfuls of spring mix
  or other mixed salad greens
1 or 2 handfuls of pea shoots
  (optional)
1 tart crisp apple, cored
  and sliced thinly
¼ cup (60 mL) pine nuts,
  lightly toasted

1 cup (250 mL) mixed sprouted
  beans (half an 8 oz/225 g
  container)
1 green onion, sliced
¼ cup (60 mL) crystallized
  ginger, sliced thinly
4 oz (125 g) Cambozola
  or brie cheese

FRESH NEW FLAVOURS keep salads fun, and fun salads get eaten. This makes a good appetizer for a main event (think Lentil & Mushroom Bourguignon, page 154), or is exactly right with a thinly sliced baguette and glass of white wine on a hot summer evening. The sprouted beans make it visually appealing, too.

TO MAKE THE DRESSING: combine all the ingredients in a small jar and shake it up. Let it sit for as long as you can, and discard the garlic clove before dressing the salad. The dressing can be made ahead of time and kept chilled (but you may want to discard the garlic sooner rather than later).

In a large bowl, toss the greens with enough dressing to just barely coat them, making sure you have a little dressing left over. Transfer the greens to 4 side plates or 2 larger plates and top with pea shoots (if using). Lay slices of apple over the greens, then distribute the pine nuts, sprouted beans, green onion, and sliced crystallized ginger evenly overtop. Lay thin slices of Cambozola on top, and drizzle a small amount of dressing over each salad. Serve immediately.

# COLD SOBA NOODLES
## *with Miso Dressing*
### SERVES 4 TO 6 AS A SIDE, OR 2 TO 3 AS A MAIN.

**DRESSING:**

1 Tbsp (15 mL) miso (shiro miso works well, but any kind would be fine)

1 Tbsp (15 mL) soy sauce

1 Tbsp (15 mL) rice vinegar

1 Tbsp (15 mL) lime juice

1 Tbsp (15 mL) sesame oil

2 Tbsp (30 mL) canola oil

¼ to ½ tsp (1 to 2.5 mL) chili sauce or chili paste

1 garlic clove, minced

½ tsp (2.5 mL) grated fresh ginger

½ tsp (2.5 mL) sugar

1 to 2 tsp (5 to 10 mL) water, if needed

**SALAD:**

6 oz (175 g) soba noodles

1 cup (250 mL) mixed sprouted beans (half an 8 oz/225 g container)

½ red pepper, julienned

1 medium carrot, shaved into strips with a vegetable peeler

2 green onions, sliced

½ cucumber, seeds removed and julienned

¼ cup (60 mL) chopped fresh cilantro

A GREAT ASIAN DRESSING on buckwheat soba and lots of crunchy sprouted beans and vegetables. This is more lime-green sundress than little black dress. If you can't find soba noodles (which are worth seeking out and can be found in most Asian or natural food markets), try whole wheat spaghetti.

TO MAKE THE DRESSING: Combine all the ingredients and taste to see if it could use a little water to thin it down. The dressing can be made ahead of time and kept chilled until ready to use.

TO MAKE THE SALAD: Cook the soba according to package directions, making sure the noodles aren't overcooked. Drain and rinse the noodles briefly under cold water and allow them to dry out slightly (blot with a clean tea towel or paper towel if you like; otherwise just shake the colander well). Tip the noodles into a large bowl and add the rest of the ingredients, except the cilantro. Add the dressing and toss well. Keep chilled until ready to eat, then top generously with cilantro.

# GREEK SALAD
## with Chickpeas & Bow-Ties
### SERVES 6 TO 8.

1 cup (250 mL) dry bow-tie pasta, or any other chunky shape

Purple onion, sliced thinly (you decide how much you want)

½ English cucumber, cut into chunks

3 to 4 Roma tomatoes, cut into chunks

2 red, orange, or yellow bell peppers, cut into chunks

½ cup (125 mL) kalamata olives

½ cup (125 mL) crumbled feta cheese

1 cup (250 mL) cooked chickpeas, or half a 19 oz (540 mL) can, rinsed and drained

½ cup (125 mL) chopped fresh flat-leaf parsley (optional)

1 to 2 chard or kale leaves, tough rib removed and remainder chopped, or a handful of torn spinach (optional)

Juice of 1 to 2 lemons

Olive oil, to taste

½ tsp (2.5 mL) minced fresh oregano or thyme

Salt and pepper to taste

NO WONDER THIS IS such a staple for barbecuing season. Every adult loves it, and it's easy for kids to deconstruct it to suit their tastes. Bow-ties make a festive sort of portable outdoor salad, but use any chunky shape—rotini or penne, for example— and as always, let quantities be dictated by your taste. Alternatively, you could dress this with any balsamic vinaigrette.

Cook the pasta according to package directions; rinse with cool water to stop the cooking and drain well.

In a large bowl, toss together the pasta, vegetables, olives, feta, chickpeas, parsley (if using), and chard. Season with the juice of 1 fresh lemon, a glug of olive oil, the oregano, and salt and pepper. Toss again and taste to see if you need more lemon, oil, or seasoning. Keep chilled until ready to serve, tossing again just before serving.

Beany, Grainy Salads

# ROASTED BEET SALAD
## *with Wild Rice, Goat Cheese & Chickpeas*
SERVES 4 TO 6.

¼ cup (60 mL) pecan pieces
or halves, toasted
1½ lb (680 g) beets, about
3 medium
½ cup (125 mL) wild rice
1 to 2 chard or kale leaves,
tough rib removed and
remainder chopped

2 green onions, sliced
1 cup (250 mL) cooked
chickpeas, or half a 19 oz
(540 mL) can, rinsed
and drained
5 oz (150 g) soft goat cheese

**DRESSING:**
⅓ cup (80 mL) olive oil
2 Tbsp (30 mL) red wine
vinegar
1 Tbsp (15 mL) balsamic vinegar
2 Tbsp (30 mL) maple syrup
1 garlic clove, crushed
Salt and pepper to taste

WE LOVE THIS SALAD at big meals, especially in the fall. It's wickedly healthy, and the colours are vibrant—saves the festive table from too many shades of brown! Roasting brings out the natural sweetness of the beets, and of course you can roast them ahead of time (tuck them into the oven while you're baking something else—multitasking at its finest). The flavours in this salad really marry well, and leftovers keep easily for a few days in the refrigerator.

Preheat the oven to 425°F. Scrub the beets and wrap them individually in tin foil. Place on a rimmed sheet and bake until tender when pierced with a knife, 1 to 1½ hours. Remove from the oven and let cool. When cool enough to handle, slip the skins off the beets (or leave them on if they're thin), and cut the roast beets into bite-sized chunks.

Bring the rice to a boil in a medium saucepan with 2 cups of water. Turn down to a simmer, cover, and cook for 35 minutes. Turn the heat off and let the rice rest covered on the stove for another 10 minutes. At this point some but not all of the grains will have split open. If you prefer all the grains open, let it rest for another 5 to 15 minutes. Drain and let cool.

TO MAKE THE DRESSING: combine the dressing ingredients in a small jar and taste for seasoning—it will be a little sweeter than most vinaigrettes. In a medium bowl, toss the beets, chard, onions, chickpeas, cooled rice, and dressing (discard garlic cloves). Transfer to a shallow dish or platter and chill until ready to serve. Scatter with pecans and bits of goat cheese right before serving.

# SPICED COUSCOUS SALAD
## *with Chickpeas*
### SERVES 6.

- 2½ cups (625 mL) low-sodium chicken or vegetable stock
- 2 cups (500 mL) couscous, regular or whole wheat
- 1 Tbsp (15 mL) grated fresh ginger
- 2 to 3 garlic cloves, crushed
- 1 tsp (5 mL) curry powder or paste
- 1 tsp (5 mL) turmeric
- ¼ tsp (1 mL) ground cinnamon

- ¼ tsp (1 mL) ground cumin
- ¼ tsp (1 mL) salt
- ½ cup (125 mL) golden raisins

- 2 cups (500 mL) cooked chickpeas, or a 19 oz (540 mL) can, rinsed and well drained
- 2 cups (500 mL) cauliflower florets

- 1 red or yellow bell pepper, seeded and chopped
- 1 cup (250 mL) sugar snap peas and/or asparagus, cut into 1-inch pieces
- Zest and juice of 1 lemon
- 2 to 4 Tbsp (30 to 60 mL) olive oil
- Parsley or cilantro for garnish (optional)

COUSCOUS IS JUST dead easy to prepare—there's no need for instant. Simmering the spices with the couscous as it cooks infuses it with flavour, minimizing the need for much in the way of dressing. The spiced couscous itself also works as a super simple side—just add the chickpeas to the mix as it absorbs the liquid, omit everything else, and serve it warm.

In a medium pot, bring the chicken stock to a boil over medium-high heat. Remove from the heat and stir in the couscous, ginger, garlic, curry, turmeric, cinnamon, cumin, and salt. Cover and let sit for 10 minutes, until all the liquid is absorbed. Fluff with a fork and dump into a bowl with the raisins. Set aside to cool.

Once the couscous has cooled, add the chickpeas and vegetables; stir in the lemon zest and squeeze the juice over the salad. Drizzle with olive oil and toss to coat. Serve immediately or refrigerate until you need it. Garnish with parsley or cilantro.

Beany, Grainy Salads

# TABBOULEH WITH BARLEY
## & Chickpeas
### SERVES 6.

⅓ cup (80 mL) pot or pearl
   barley
2 to 3 cups (500 to 750 mL)
   packed chopped fresh
   parsley (about 1 large bunch)
4 green onions, sliced thinly
¼ cup (60 mL) chopped
   fresh mint

2 Roma tomatoes, seeded
   and chopped
1 cup (250 mL) cooked
   chickpeas, or half a 19 oz
   (540 mL) can, rinsed and
   drained

**DRESSING:**
4 to 6 Tbsp (60 to 90 mL)
   fresh lemon juice, according
   to your taste
¼ cup (60 mL) olive oil
¼ tsp (1 mL) salt
Freshly ground black pepper
   to taste

WHILE BULGUR IS traditionally used in tabbouleh, we've discovered that barley substitutes beautifully. The chickpeas also seem right at home, like they've never been anywhere else. If you'd prefer to use bulgur, soak the same quantity in two to three times its volume of cold water until it's tender, then squeeze out any excess water.

Cook the barley in 1 cup of water in a small covered saucepan until tender, about 40 minutes. Drain excess water if necessary and set aside to cool.

Combine the dressing ingredients in a medium bowl. Add the parsley, green onions, mint, tomatoes, and chickpeas. Add the cooled barley and toss everything well to combine. Adjust the seasoning and add a little more lemon if you like. The tabbouleh is best chilled for at least an hour before serving, and keeps well in the refrigerator for a few days.

Beany, Grainy Salads

# LENTIL & WILD RICE SALAD

### SERVES 8 TO 10.

½ cup (125 mL) dry green,
brown or du Puy lentils
½ cup (125 mL) wild rice
2 celery stalks
1 red bell pepper
2 to 3 Roma tomatoes
½ English cucumber

4 to 5 green onions, sliced
¼ cup (60 mL) chopped fresh
dill, or 1 Tbsp (15 mL) dried
¼ cup (60 mL) chopped
fresh parsley
5 oz (150 g) feta cheese,
crumbled

2 carrots, grated
Juice of 1 to 2 lemons
½ tsp (2.5 mL) sugar
¼ cup (60 mL) olive oil
Salt and pepper to taste

ONE OF THOSE SALADS that makes heaps, but keeps really well in the refrigerator. You can dip into it for lunches and after going to the gym, and bring it back to the supper table the next night. As with most recipes of this nature, the proportions and ingredients are extremely fluid. The wild rice keeps the texture that little bit crunchy, but feel free to substitute brown rice or omit it altogether. If you need to feed a crowd, keep the wild rice but bolster the salad with some whole wheat couscous. French du Puy lentils look pretty here, but others work fine, too.

In a medium saucepan, cook the lentils in 2 cups of water until soft but not mushy, about 30 to 40 minutes. If the pan is in danger of drying out before the lentils are cooked, add more water as needed, about ½ cup at a time. Set aside to cool, then transfer to a large bowl.

In a second medium saucepan, boil the rice with 2 cups of water. Turn down to a simmer and cook, covered, for 35 minutes. Turn the heat off and let the rice rest covered on the stove for another 10 minutes. At this point some but not all of the grains will have split open. If you prefer all the grains open, let it rest for another 5 to 15 minutes. Drain and cool, then add to the lentils (both rice and lentils can be cooked the night before and kept chilled until you're ready to proceed).

Chop the celery, pepper, tomatoes, and cucumber into chunks about ¼ to ½ inch square and add to the bowl with the rice and lentils. Add the green onions, herbs, feta, carrots, juice of 1 lemon, sugar, olive oil, and black pepper to taste. Give the salad a good toss; add more lemon if you like, and salt if you think it's needed. Chill and serve.

# WHITE BEAN & TUNA PASTA SALAD

## SERVES 6 TO 8.

2 cups (500 mL) dry rotini or
other small pasta
2 cups (500 mL) cooked white
beans, or a 19 oz (540 mL)
can, rinsed and drained
6 oz (170 g) can tuna, drained

1 to 2 celery stalks, chopped
(leafy parts too)
¼ cup (60 mL) chopped fresh
parsley and/or basil

**DRESSING:**
¼ cup (60 mL) olive oil
3 Tbsp (45 mL) red wine
or balsamic vinegar
1 garlic clove, crushed
Salt and pepper to taste

A HARD-BOILED (OR soft-boiled) egg or two is delicious chopped into this salad, which transports well and keeps in the refrigerator without wilting. Grape tomatoes, chunked artichoke hearts, or pitted olives make fine accessories, too. If you start with dry beans, simmer them with a clove of garlic and a bay leaf or sprig of rosemary in the water to boost flavour.

Cook the pasta according to package directions; run under cool water and drain well, then transfer to a bowl. Add the beans, flake in the tuna, then add the celery, parsley, and/ or basil.

In a small jar or bowl, shake or whisk together the oil, vinegar, and garlic; drizzle over the salad and toss to coat. Season with salt and freshly ground pepper and serve, or refrigerate until needed.

# PANZANELLA SALAD

SERVES 4 TO 6.

½ loaf crusty bread or baguette, cut or torn into chunks

½ lb (250 g) green beans, trimmed

2 cups (500 mL) cooked white beans, or a 19 oz (540 mL) can, rinsed and drained

½ to 1 lb (250 to 500 g) mozzarella cheese, diced

2 cups (500 mL) grape or cherry tomatoes, halved (about a pint)

½ small purple onion, finely chopped

½ cup (125 mL) pitted kalamata olives

Handful of torn fresh basil or flat-leaf parsley

1 Tbsp (15 mL) capers, drained (optional)

Freshly ground black pepper to taste

**DRESSING:**

½ cup (125 mL) canola or olive oil, plus extra if needed

¼ cup (60 mL) red wine vinegar

¼ cup (60 mL) lemon juice

2 tsp (10 mL) grainy Dijon mustard

THIS CRUSTY CROUTON-based salad can easily be transformed into a pan bagnat (pahn bahn-YAHT, a fancy name for a French sandwich composed of niçoise salad ingredients) salad by adding a chopped hard-boiled egg and a can of tuna. If you like, top with wide shavings of Parmigiano Reggiano cheese, made all dramatic-looking by using a vegetable peeler.

If you like, spread the bread chunks out on a baking sheet, drizzle with oil, and toast in a 400°F oven until golden. Blanch the green beans in a pot of boiling water for a minute or two, then plunge into a bowl of cold water to stop them from cooking. Drain well and pat dry with paper towels, so that they don't sog out the croutons.

Put the toasted croutons (or fresh bread chunks) into a wide bowl with the green beans, white beans, mozzarella, tomatoes, onion, olives, basil, and capers (if using). Grind fresh pepper overtop.

In a jar or small bowl, shake or stir together the oil, vinegar, lemon juice, and mustard; drizzle over the salad and toss with tongs to coat. Serve immediately.

# Sandwiches

# FALAFEL

MAKES ABOUT 20 FALAFEL BALLS OR PATTIES.

| | | |
|---|---|---|
| 2 cups (500 mL) rinsed and drained canned chickpeas (19 oz/540 mL can) | 2 Tbsp (30 mL) chopped fresh parsley | Pinch of dried red chili flakes |
| 1 small onion, chopped | 2 Tbsp (30 mL) chopped fresh cilantro | ¼ cup (60 mL) all-purpose or whole wheat flour (plus extra if needed) |
| 2 to 4 garlic cloves, peeled | 1 tsp (5 mL) ground cumin | 1 tsp (5 mL) baking powder |
| | ¼ tsp (1 mL) salt | Canola oil, for frying |

HUMMUS HAS BEEN A bit of a staple in both of our houses—it's so easy to blitz together in the food processor using a can of chickpeas. Turns out the process is almost the same to make falafel—you just don't want to go quite as far and turn your ingredients into a dip. Feel free to adjust ingredients or try adding new stuff, just as you would with hummus, and use brown rice or chickpea flour if you want gluten-free falafel. If there are leftovers, use them to stuff your next roasted chicken. (Brilliant, no?) Adapted from a recipe in Joan Nathan's *The Foods of Israel Today.*

Put the chickpeas, onion, garlic, parsley, cilantro, cumin, salt, and chili flakes in the bowl of a food processor and pulse until combined but still chunky. Add the flour and baking powder and pulse until you have a soft mixture that you can roll into balls without it sticking to your hands. (Add another spoonful or so of flour if you need to.) Roll the dough into meatball-sized balls, and if you like, flatten each into a little patty. We like doing this for maximum surface area, which equals more crunch. (They also cook through more quickly as the distance between the middle and exterior is shorter.)

In a shallow pot or skillet, heat about ½ inch of canola oil until it's hot but not smoking. Test it with a bit of falafel mixture or a scrap of bread—the oil should bubble up around it. Cook the falafel for a few minutes per side, without crowding the pan (which will cool down the oil), until they're nicely golden. (You could get away with using just a skiff of oil—if you do this, best to leave the falafel round, so that you can roll them around in the pan to brown all sides.) Transfer to paper towels.

Serve in pitas with tzatziki, chopped cucumber, purple onion, and tomato.

# CRISPY BLACK BEAN TACOS
## *with Feta & Slaw*
### SERVES 6 TO 8.

2 cups (500 mL) rinsed and
   drained canned black beans
   (19 oz/540 mL can)
⅓ cup (80 mL) salsa (optional)
1 green onion, chopped
   (optional)
1 tsp (5 mL) chili powder

½ tsp (2.5 mL) ground cumin
Salt to taste
2 cups (500 mL) bagged
   coleslaw or finely chopped
   cabbage
⅓ cup (80 mL) chopped
   fresh cilantro

2 Tbsp (30 mL) olive or canola
   oil or mayo
1 Tbsp (15 mL) lime juice
Canola or olive oil, for cooking
6–8 small corn or flour tortillas
½ cup (125 mL) crumbled
   feta cheese

THANKS TO THE February 2009 issue of *Bon Appétit* for inspiring this one—it's fast and easy, and a great use of canned refried beans if you want to swap them for the do-it-yourself seasoned black beans. To make this recipe into great tasting burritos, stuff flour tortillas with beans, salsa, slaw, and feta, then wrap and cook in a skillet until golden and crisp.

In a small bowl, roughly mash the black beans, salsa (if using), green onion (if using), chili powder, cumin, and salt. In another bowl, toss the coleslaw with the cilantro, oil or mayo, and lime juice.

Heat a drizzle of oil in a heavy skillet set over medium-high heat. Divide the bean mixture among the tortillas, filling each about one-third full, and fold in half; add to the pan 2 at a time and cook until golden brown on each side, adding more oil and flipping as you need to. Stuff them with feta and slaw and serve immediately.

**NOTE:**
For quick, DIY refried beans, sauté a crushed garlic clove in a drizzle of oil, add a drained can of pinto beans (or another variety if you prefer), and mash them in the pan with a fork or a potato masher. Throw in a pinch or two of chili powder if you like!

# BLACK BEAN QUESADILLAS
## SERVES 6 TO 8.

6 to 8 flour tortillas
   (any variety)
2 cups (500 mL) shredded
   cheddar, Gouda, or
   Monterey Jack cheese

1 cup (250 mL) cooked black,
   white, or pinto beans, or half
   a 19 oz (540 mL) can, rinsed
   and drained
1 fresh mango or 1 to 2 plum
   tomatoes, finely chopped

¼ to ½ cup (60 to 125 mL)
   finely chopped purple or
   green onion
¼ to ½ cup (60 to 125 mL)
   chopped fresh cilantro
   (optional)

YOU CAN PUT ANY-thing you like inside these quesadillas—peppers, mushrooms, shredded chicken, or crumbled sausage (they make great use of leftovers). To prevent a mess while flipping, make half-moon quesadillas out of a single tortilla folded in half; once the cheese melts it will glue the sides together and you can flip it across the fold, keeping everything intact.

Working with one tortilla at a time, fold it in half, then open again and sprinkle one side with grated cheese, beans, mango or tomatoes, onion, and cilantro (if using), keeping the filling from getting too close to the edge. Sprinkle with a little more cheese to ensure the tortilla sticks on both sides. Close the tortilla like a book.

TO COOK ON THE STOVETOP: Heat a heavy skillet over medium-high heat; if you like, add a drizzle of canola or olive oil—this will make them crispy, but it isn't necessary. Cook one quesadilla at a time, flipping as the bottom turns golden and the cheese melts. Cook until golden on the other side.

TO GRILL: Preheat your grill to medium-high and gently place the quesadillas, a few at a time, directly on it; close the lid for a minute or two. When the cheese has melted and the quesadillas are crispy and golden on the bottom, turn them over with tongs, flipping them across the folded edge. Cook for another minute, until golden on the other side.

Cut into wedges and serve with salsa and sour cream.

# BEET & BLACK BEAN BURGERS

### MAKES 6 TO 8 BURGERS; MORE IF THEY'RE SMALLER PATTIES.

Canola or olive oil, for cooking

1 small onion, grated on the coarse side of a box grater

1 large red beet, peeled and grated on the coarse side of a box grater

3 garlic cloves, crushed

½ tsp (2.5 mL) ground cumin

1 Tbsp (15 mL) balsamic vinegar

2 cups (500 mL) rinsed and drained canned black beans (19 oz/540 mL can)

1 cup (250 mL) freshly cooked brown rice, barley, or quinoa

2 Tbsp (30 mL) chopped fresh parsley or cilantro

Salt and pepper to taste

Provolone, Gouda, or other mild, meltable cheese, shredded or thinly sliced (optional)

Butter or leaf lettuce leaves (optional)

Tzatziki, for serving (optional)

HONESTLY, THESE ARE far more delicious than they sound. Truly. Trust us here. Make sure the rice is freshly cooked and sticky; once cooled the grains tend to separate and not be as starchy, so the burgers will have a tougher time holding together. These are fun made small, then wrapped in lettuce leaves and topped with tzatziki, but you could of course load them on a regular burger bun, full-sized or slider-sized, as well. We most often eat them straight up, from the pan, with our fingers.

In a medium skillet, heat a drizzle of oil over medium-high heat and cook the onion for a few minutes, until soft. Add the grated beet, garlic, cumin, and vinegar; stir and cover; cook for about 5 minutes, until the beet is softened.

In a large bowl or the bowl of a food processor, combine the black beans, rice, parsley, salt and pepper, and cooked beet mixture. Mash with a potato masher or pulse in the food processor until the mixture is partly mashed and well combined but still chunky—you don't want to purée it completely.

Heat a generous drizzle of oil in a heavy skillet set over medium-high heat. Shape the mixture into patties (large or small) and cook for a few minutes per side, allowing them to develop a nice crust on the bottom before you flip them. If you like, place a piece of cheese on top after the first flip, then cover for a few minutes to help the cheese melt.

Serve on regular-sized or little slider-sized buns (see page 224), or omit the cheese and serve with lettuce leaves; have everyone put a patty on a lettuce leaf, top with tzatziki, wrap, and eat.

*Spilling the Beans*

# LENTIL & WALNUT BURGERS

## MAKES ABOUT 6 PATTIES.

2 cups (500 mL) rinsed and drained canned lentils (19 oz/540 mL can)

1 cup (250 mL) walnut or pecan halves or pieces, toasted

1 small onion, chopped

1 garlic clove, chopped

2 large eggs

Salt and pepper to taste

2 cups (500 mL) breadcrumbs

Canola or olive oil, for cooking

TO US, A BURGER IS A burger and beany vegetarian burgers should not attempt to taste like meat. Because lentils aren't meat, right? Which isn't to say they aren't delicious just as their healthy legumey selves. But what do you call a patty of lentils and walnuts if not a burger? Use dry or fresh breadcrumbs in these—dry crumbs will absorb more moisture, and fresh will produce a softer mixture. Make sure to use canned lentils—they are softer and easier to process. Go to town with various spices, too—cumin, curry, herbs; lentils and walnuts get on well with all sorts of flavours.

In the bowl of a food processor, combine the lentils, walnuts, onion, garlic, eggs, and salt and pepper. Pulse until well blended but not completely smooth, scraping down the sides of the bowl once or twice. Pour into a bowl and stir in the breadcrumbs. Let the mixture sit for about half an hour (this will give the crumbs a chance to plump up and absorb any excess moisture).

In a large, heavy skillet, heat a drizzle of oil over medium-high heat. Shape the lentil mixture into patties and cook in batches until golden on the bottom; flip and cook for another minute or two, until golden on the other side. Serve as is, or on buns with mayo, lettuce, and tomatoes.

# TURKEY CHICKPEA SLIDERS

MAKES ABOUT 8 SMALL PATTIES.

1 cup (250 mL) cooked
  chickpeas, or half a 19 oz
  (540 mL) can, rinsed and
  drained
⅛ tsp (0.5 mL) dried rosemary
⅛ tsp (0.5 mL) dried thyme
Pinch of ground fennel seed
½ lb (250 g) ground turkey
  (thigh meat if you have
  the choice)

1 large egg
¼ cup (60 mL) dry
  breadcrumbs
2 garlic cloves
1 Tbsp (15 mL) chopped
  fresh parsley
2 Tbsp (30 mL) grated
  Parmesan cheese
1 green onion, chopped fine

Pinch of cayenne pepper
  or a dash or 2 of hot sauce
  (optional)
¼ tsp (1 mL) salt, plus a little
  more to taste if you like
Big grind of black pepper

Oil, for frying
Buns (see page 224)

SLIDERS MAKE SO much sense to us: when you're eating mini-burgers you don't need to commit to dressing them just one way. You can have two! Or three! Sliders make great party food. You can also eat the patties broken into two or three pieces and used like falafel in pita bread, or shape the mix into meatballs for any use you like.

Start by very coarsely mashing the chickpeas with a fork—don't turn them into a paste, and don't use a food processor or you'll wind up with purée. Crush the rosemary, thyme, and fennel seed together with a mortar and pestle or rub it between your fingers.

Combine all the ingredients in a medium bowl and gently combine with your hands, taking care not to overwork the mixture. To test for seasoning, take a pinch of the combined mix and cook it, then taste. Adjust the seasonings as you see fit, and then shape into patties about ½ inch thick and 2½ inches in diameter, or whatever will match the buns. Fry in batches until nicely browned and cooked through, or cook on the grill using a grill basket. Slide onto buns and dress accordingly.

# NEW-SCHOOL TUNA MELTS

MAKES 4 TUNA MELTS.

1 cup (250 mL) rinsed and drained canned white beans (half a 19 oz/540 mL can)
1 garlic clove, crushed
2 to 4 Tbsp (30 to 60 mL) extra-virgin olive oil
2 Tbsp (30 mL) lemon juice

6 oz (170 g) can tuna, drained
1 celery stalk, finely chopped
¼ cup (60 mL) pitted kalamata olives, finely chopped
2 Tbsp (30 mL) chopped fresh basil or flat-leaf parsley, or a combination

Salt and pepper to taste
4 slices thick, grainy bread
1 cup (250 mL) shredded old cheddar, Gouda, or any other cheese you like

DITCH THE MAYO AND boost fibre and nutrients by adding canned white beans to your regular tuna sandwich; garlic, olive oil, fresh herbs, and olives ensure there's no loss in the flavour department. If you prefer a straight-up sandwich to a melt, stuff the tuna filling between two slices of bread (or into a pita or bun) with lettuce and tomato, and ditch the cheese.

In a medium bowl, combine the beans, garlic, a drizzle of oil, and lemon juice, and roughly mash with a fork. Flake in the tuna, then stir in the celery, olives, basil and/or parsley, and salt and pepper.

Toast the bread and place on a baking sheet; top each slice with the bean mixture, spreading it to the edges. Scatter with the grated cheese. Broil for a few minutes, just until the cheese melts.

# CHICKPEA MASALA SANDWICHES
## (Doubles)
### SERVES 4 TO 8.

**FLATBREAD:**

2 cups (500 mL) all-purpose
flour

1 tsp (5 mL) active dry yeast

1 tsp (5 mL) turmeric (optional)

½ tsp (2.5 mL) ground cumin

½ tsp (2.5 mL) sugar

¼ tsp (1 mL) salt

Canola oil, for cooking

**FILLING:**

1 large onion, halved and
thinly sliced

1 Tbsp (15 mL) curry powder
or paste, or to taste

2 cups (500 mL) cooked
chickpeas, or a 19 oz
(540 mL) can, rinsed
and drained

3 garlic cloves, crushed

¼ cup (60 mL) chopped fresh
cilantro, or to taste

1 cup (250 mL) chicken or
vegetable stock or water

Mango or other chutney,
for serving

A POPULAR INDIAN street food, doubles are made with flatbread filled with braised spiced chickpeas. They are ridiculously good—so worth the effort of making from scratch. Try cooking mini flatbreads (the size of a mini pita) to serve alongside the filling at parties—a sort of do-it-yourself mini double. This version was inspired by/adapted from the *Naparima Girls' High School Cookbook*.

In a large bowl, stir together the flour, yeast, turmeric (if using), cumin, sugar, and salt; add ¾ cup of warm water and stir until the dough comes together. On a lightly floured surface, knead the dough for about 5 minutes, until it's smooth and elastic. Return the dough to the bowl, cover it with a tea towel or plastic wrap, and set it aside for about an hour, until it doubles in size.

TO MAKE THE FILLING: heat a drizzle of oil in a large, heavy skillet set over medium-high heat. Sauté the onion for about 5 minutes, until soft; add the curry powder or paste and cook for a few more minutes. Add the chickpeas, garlic, and cilantro and cook, stirring, for a minute or two, then pour the stock or water overtop and bring to a simmer. Turn the heat down to medium-low, partially cover, and cook for about an hour, until the chickpeas are very soft.

TO COOK THE FLATBREADS: divide the dough into
12 balls and roll each one out very thin on a lightly floured
surface (or between 2 sheets of waxed paper), into circles
that are about 8 inches in diameter (they don't have to be
perfect!). You can roll them all at once, or roll each one
before cooking it.

Heat a generous drizzle of oil in a heavy skillet set over
medium-high heat and cook the breads one at a time,
turning with tongs, until puffed and golden, about a
minute each. Transfer to paper towels to cool while you
cook the remaining dough.

Spoon the spiced chickpeas onto the flatbreads and top with
chutney and extra cilantro, if you like; wrap and eat hot.

# Soups & Stews

# CHICKEN NOODLE SOUP

### SERVES 6 TO 8.

1 Tbsp (15 mL) olive or
  vegetable oil
1 Tbsp (15 mL) butter
1 medium onion, diced
1 celery stalk, diced
1 carrot, diced
2 garlic cloves, minced
¼ cup (60 mL) red lentils
¼ cup (60 mL) pearl or
  pot barley

½ tsp (2.5 mL) turmeric
  (optional)
8 cups (2 L) chicken or
  vegetable stock
2 cups (500 mL) cooked white
  beans, or a 19 oz (540 mL)
  can, rinsed and drained
1 skinless, boneless chicken
  breast or 2 thighs (about
  ½ lb/250 g)

1½ cups (375 mL) chopped
  broccoli (florets quite small,
  about fingertip size, tough
  outer stems removed)
1½ cups (375 mL) dry pasta
  (egg noodles are traditional,
  but any kind will do)
Salt and pepper to taste
Fresh cilantro or parsley,
  chopped (optional)

WE'VE ADDED WHITE beans, barley, and red lentils to a basic chicken noodle soup to boost nutrition while keeping the essential character of the soup intact. Poaching the entire chicken breast in the soup before cutting it up ensures the chicken is cooked gently, keeping it tender and flavourful. Always much preferred over nasty and rubbery, which can happen if the chicken is boiled. Feel free to use skinless chicken thighs, which are less expensive and tend to have more flavour than chicken breast, and not much more fat. Turmeric is optional but will add a lovely colour.

Heat the olive oil and butter in a large soup pot set over medium heat and sauté the onion, celery, and carrot until softened slightly, about 5 to 8 minutes. Add the garlic and a little salt and pepper and sauté for another 1 to 2 minutes. Add the lentils, barley, turmeric (if using), stock, and beans. Bring just to a boil, reduce the heat, and simmer gently until the barley is cooked, about 40 minutes.

Remove the pot from the heat and slip the whole chicken breast into the partially finished soup. Cover and, leaving the pot off the heat, set a timer for 10 minutes. At the end of 10 minutes, fish out the chicken breast with a pair of tongs and remove to a plate. (If it's not quite cooked through, don't fret: as soon as it's cut up and returned to the pot it will finish cooking almost immediately.)

Return the soup to the burner and bring it back to a boil. Add the pasta and set the timer for about 3 minutes less than you expect the pasta will need to cook (check the package directions). While the pasta cooks, either dice or shred the slightly cooled chicken. When the timer goes off, return the chicken to the soup and add the broccoli. Cook for another 2 to 3 minutes, checking the pasta, broccoli, and chicken for doneness, and adjusting the seasoning if needed. Ladle into bowls, and top with cilantro or parsley if you wish.

# BLACK BEAN SOUP

## SERVES 6 TO 8.

Canola or olive oil, for cooking
1 onion, peeled and chopped
1 carrot, peeled and chopped
2 celery stalks, chopped
   (including the leafy parts!)
1 jalapeño pepper, seeded
   and minced, or 1 tsp (5 mL)
   chopped canned chipotle
   chilies
4 garlic cloves, crushed

1 small red or yellow bell
   pepper, chopped
2 tsp (10 mL) ground cumin
2 cups (500 mL) cooked black
   beans, or a 19 oz (540 mL)
   can, rinsed and drained
12 oz (341 mL) can kernel corn,
   drained, or kernels scraped
   from 1 to 2 fresh corn cobs
   (optional)

14 oz (398 mL) or 28 oz
   (796 mL) can diced or
   stewed tomatoes, undrained
4 cups (1 L) chicken or
   vegetable stock
Salt and pepper to taste

Sour cream, chopped cilantro,
   chopped green onions, and/
   or crumbled feta cheese
   (optional)

THIS SOUP IMPROVES in flavour (and spiciness) after a day or two in the refrigerator, so make it ahead if you can. To make it a little more substantial, put a scoop of rice into each bowl and ladle the soup over it. A crumbled spicy Italian sausage or bit of diced ham is also delicious—sauté either along with the onion at the beginning. This cooks the sausage, of course, but also allows the sausage (or the ham) to flavour the entire pot of soup, which doesn't happen if it is thrown in at the end.

Heat the oil in a large saucepan set over medium-high heat and sauté the onion, carrot, and celery for about 5 minutes, until they begin to soften. Add the jalapeño, garlic, red pepper, and cumin and cook for another minute. Add the beans, corn (if using), tomatoes, and chicken stock. Bring the soup to a boil, reduce the heat to low, cover, and cook for 15 to 20 minutes, until the carrot is tender.

If you like, you could use a blender, food processor, or handheld immersion blender to process about half of the soup until smooth, then return it to the pot. (Process as much or as little of the soup as you want to make the consistency as chunky or smooth as you like, or leave it all chunky.) Turn the heat down and simmer the soup uncovered for half an hour or so to allow it to thicken slightly. Season with salt and pepper.

Serve hot, topped with a dollop of sour cream and a sprinkle of cilantro, green onions, and/or feta cheese.

# CREAMY MUSHROOM SOUP
## *with Little White Beans*
### SERVES 4 TO 6.

¾ lb (350 g) mushrooms (button, shiitake, cremini, oyster, portobello, or a combination)—about 4 cups

Canola or olive oil, for cooking

1 to 2 Tbsp (15 to 30 mL) butter

1 small onion, peeled and finely chopped

1 to 2 garlic cloves, crushed

½ cup (125 mL) chopped ham (optional)

3 Tbsp (45 mL) sherry or brandy (optional)

1 Tbsp (15 mL) flour

4 cups (1 L) chicken, beef, or vegetable stock

1 cup (250 mL) cooked white beans, or half a 19 oz (540 mL) can, rinsed and drained

½ cup (125 mL) half-and-half or whipping cream

Salt and pepper to taste

CREAM OF MUSHROOM soup has been Sue's favourite since we were kids. As a teenager she, the more mature of the two of us, would always order soup at restaurants while I (Julie) ordered fries and gravy. Button mushrooms are fine to use in a cream of mushroom soup, and it's a great way to use them up if they are starting to wither and dry out. Try meatier portobello mushrooms and exotic varieties such as shiitake, oyster, and cremini to give it more substance and an intense mushroom flavour. To make a vegetarian soup, leave out the ham and use vegetable stock.

Clean the mushrooms and slice half of them. Finely chop the other half. Heat a drizzle of oil in a large saucepan set over medium-high heat, and add the butter. When the foam subsides, add the onion, garlic, and both sliced and chopped mushrooms and sauté until the moisture evaporates and the mushrooms begin to turn golden.

Add the ham (if using) and cook for a minute. Add the sherry (if using) and cook until it evaporates, then add the flour and cook, stirring to coat the mushrooms, for another minute. Add the stock and beans and bring to a simmer. Reduce the heat to low and cook for about 15 minutes.

Turn off the heat and stir in the cream. Season with salt and pepper and serve immediately.

# MULLIGATAWNY SOUP

## SERVES 6 TO 8.

1 small roasted chicken (a deli rotisserie chicken works well)

1 onion

Canola or olive oil, for cooking

2 carrots, peeled and chopped

2 celery stalks, chopped

1 jalapeño pepper, seeded and finely chopped

3 garlic cloves, crushed or chopped

1 Tbsp (15 mL) grated fresh ginger

1 Tbsp (15 mL) curry paste or powder

1 tsp (5 mL) ground cumin

2 cups (500 mL) cooked chickpeas, or a 19 oz (540 mL) can, rinsed and drained

1 tsp (5 mL) salt

14 oz (398 mL) can coconut milk (optional)

1 tart apple (such as Granny Smith), cored and finely chopped

Steamed rice, for serving

Chopped fresh cilantro and/or chopped salted peanuts, for garnish (optional)

MULLIGATAWNY IS A rich, curried chicken soup that takes on chickpeas very well. It makes great use of a deli roast chicken. Next time you roast a chicken, roast two and set one aside to make mulligatawny, or just use the leftovers from one roast chicken if you don't care how meaty it is.

To serve, put a scoop of steamed rice in the bottom of each serving bowl and ladle the soup overtop. If you like tomatoes in your mulligatawny, add a 19 oz can of diced or stewed tomatoes along with (or instead of) the coconut milk.

Pull the meat off the roasted chicken, discarding the skin (we feed ours to the dog—no, we totally don't eat it ourselves while no one's looking) and putting the carcass and bones into a saucepan. Set the meat aside and just barely cover the carcass with water. Peel the onion and add the outer layers of skin to the pan. Bring to a simmer and cook for about half an hour. Strain into a bowl or pot and set aside. You should have 4 to 6 cups of stock.

Meanwhile, chop the onion and sauté it in a drizzle of oil in a large soup pot set over medium-high heat. Add the carrots, celery, jalapeño, garlic, and ginger and cook for a few minutes, until soft. Add the curry paste, cumin, and chickpeas and cook for another minute or two.

Add the chicken stock, salt, and chopped chicken and bring to a simmer. Cook for about 10 minutes, then add the coconut milk (if using) and apple and heat through.

Put a scoop of rice into each bowl and ladle the soup overtop. If you like, sprinkle with cilantro and/or chopped peanuts.

# ITALIAN VEGETABLE STEW

SERVES 6; MORE IF YOU USE ADDITIONAL INGREDIENTS.

**BASIC STEW:**

Canola or olive oil, for cooking

1 purple onion, coarsely chopped

1 carrot, halved lengthwise and sliced thinly

2 garlic cloves, minced

28 oz (796 mL) can diced tomatoes with their juices

1 red bell pepper, coarsely chopped

¾ lb (375 g) red- or yellow-skinned potatoes, skin left on, chopped

2 small zucchini, cut in half lengthwise and sliced thinly

1 to 2 cups (250 to 500 mL) cooked chickpeas, or half to a full 19 oz (540 mL) can, rinsed and drained

**OPTIONAL ADDITIONS:**

1 celery stalk, halved lengthwise and sliced thinly

1 small eggplant, chopped

¼ lb (125 g) green or yellow beans, cut into pieces

6 asparagus stalks, snapped in pieces

½ bunch chard, coarse stems discarded and leaves shredded

1 to 2 Italian sausages, meat squeezed out into tiny meatballs (can be browned in the oven first, or dropped straight into the hot stew to simmer once the zucchini is cooked)

THIS IS QUITE similar to a ratatouille, without the herbs. The basic stew is bold and simple, resulting in a fresh and satisfying meal. Adjust the ingredients according to what's fresh and seasonal, and of course to your taste preferences. The focaccia on page 230 pairs beautifully here.

In a large saucepan or Dutch oven set over medium heat, heat a drizzle of oil and sauté the onion, carrot, and celery (if using) for about 5 minutes, until just starting to soften and brown. Add the garlic and cook for 1 more minute, then add the tomatoes, pepper, potatoes, and eggplant (if using).

Cover and simmer until the potatoes are tender, 20 to 25 minutes. Add the zucchini and chickpeas (plus the asparagus, green or yellow beans, and Italian sausage, if using), and simmer until all the vegetables are cooked. (If you've added raw sausage, ensure it is cooked through.) If you are using chard, sauté it in a little oil, in a separate pan, over medium-high heat before adding it to the pot. Dish up the stew and serve immediately.

# ITALIAN THREESOME

### SERVES 6 TO 8.

Canola or olive oil, for cooking

1 large onion, finely chopped

1 carrot, cut in half lengthwise and thinly sliced

3 garlic cloves, minced

8 cups (2 L) chicken stock

2 cups (500 mL) cooked white beans, or a 19 oz (540 mL) can, rinsed and drained

1 lb (500 g) fresh Italian sausages

⅔ cup (160 mL) dry orzo or other small pasta

2 cups (500 mL) chopped fresh spinach or chard

2 eggs

¼ cup (60 mL) grated Parmesan cheese, plus more for the table

Salt and pepper to taste

THIS IS A BEANY RIFF on Italian Wedding, a traditional soup with pasta and meatballs. The beans fit right in—certainly an equal player, so why not make it a threesome? As with most soups that contain pasta, it's best to add the pasta right before you serve this.

Preheat the oven to 350°F.

Heat a drizzle of oil in a large soup pot set over medium heat, and sauté the onion and carrot with a pinch of salt until they're softened and starting to brown, 4 to 6 minutes. Add the garlic and cook for another minute. Add the stock and white beans and bring to a simmer. Simmer for 20 minutes.

In the meantime, spray a large rimmed baking sheet with non-stick cooking spray. Cut a small hole in the end of each sausage casing, then squeeze out the sausage meat teaspoon by teaspoon and place on the sheet, making tiny meatballs (no need to roll them). Bake the meatballs, shaking the pan once or twice, until nicely browned. Transfer the browned meatballs to the soup along with the pasta and spinach. Simmer until the pasta is nearly tender, 6 to 7 minutes.

While the pasta is cooking, lightly beat the 2 eggs in a small bowl, stir in the Parmesan, and season with salt and pepper. Just before serving, stir the soup briskly, pouring the eggs into the centre of the pot in a thin stream. Taste for seasoning and then ladle into bowls. Pass around additional Parmesan at the table.

# LEBANESE SPINACH & LENTIL SOUP

## SERVES 4.

Canola or olive oil, for cooking
1 large onion, finely chopped
4 garlic cloves, minced
3 cups (750 mL) water
4 cups (1 L) chicken or
  vegetable stock

1 cup (250 mL) lentils (French
  blue ones are nice here;
  green would be fine, too)
2 tsp (10 mL) ground cumin
½ tsp (2.5 mL) ground
  cinnamon
10 oz (300 g) package frozen
  spinach, thawed

3 oz (90 g) dry vermicelli or
  other fine pasta, broken
Juice of ½ to 1 lemon
Salt and pepper to taste
¼ cup (60 mL) chopped
  fresh cilantro

A TRADITIONAL SOUP, this is just as delicious made with fresh chard swapped for the spinach, or mint swapped for the cilantro. A tomato salad makes a fine partner, and bread with tzatziki will round things off nicely.

In a large saucepan set over low-moderate heat, sauté the onion in a drizzle of oil with a pinch of salt until transparent and starting to brown, 4 to 7 minutes. Add the garlic and cook for 1 more minute. Add the water, stock, lentils, and spices, and bring to a simmer. Cook, covered, until the lentils are tender, 30 to 40 minutes.

In the meantime, drain the spinach in a colander and squeeze by handfuls to remove as much liquid as possible. In a large skillet, sauté the spinach in batches with a drizzle of olive oil and a pinch of salt until cooked and almost crisp. Transfer the cooked spinach to a plate and set aside.

Once the lentils are tender, add the vermicelli pieces and cook until the pasta is nearly tender, about 4 to 6 minutes. Add the sautéed spinach and juice of half a lemon to the pot, stir well, and add salt and pepper. Add more lemon if you like, or pass around wedges at the table. Ladle into bowls and top with cilantro.

# MINESTRONE
## SERVES 8.

Canola or olive oil, for cooking
1 small onion, diced
1 garlic clove, minced
¼ lb (125 g) pancetta or
  bacon, diced
4 cups (1 L) chicken or
  vegetable stock
14 oz (398 mL) can whole
  or diced tomatoes, or 2 large
  tomatoes, diced

2 medium red or Yukon Gold
  potatoes (peeling optional)
1 carrot, cut in half lengthwise
  and sliced thinly crosswise
2 small or 1 large zucchini,
  diced
¼ lb (125 g) green beans,
  cut into bite-sized pieces
2 cups (500 mL) any kind
  of cooked beans, or a 19 oz

(540 mL) can, rinsed
  and drained
small head napa or Savoy
  cabbage (or even bok choy),
  sliced thinly
⅓ cup (80 mL) pesto, plus
  more for the table if you wish
1 cup (250 mL) dry pasta,
  cooked about 3 minutes
  less than package indicates
Salt and pepper to taste

THERE ARE AS MANY versions of minestrone as there are cooks. It's really all about using what's available, either at the markets or in your refrigerator or pantry. If you anticipate leftovers, make only enough pasta for the first night. Add it directly to the serving bowls and then ladle the soup on top.

Heat a drizzle of oil in a large saucepan or Dutch oven, and sauté the onion, garlic, and pancetta or bacon until the onion is transparent, about 5 minutes. Add the stock and tomatoes and bring to a simmer. Add the potatoes, carrot, zucchini, both types of beans, and cabbage to the pot, and simmer again. Cook, uncovered, until the vegetables are tender, about 30 minutes.

Add the pesto and pasta right before serving, and taste for seasoning (you may not need any—both the pancetta and pesto are quite salty). Pass around more pesto at the table if you wish.

# ROASTED PARSNIP SOUP

## SERVES 4 TO 6.

1¼ lb (625 g) parsnips (about 5; 4 to bake and 1 for the chips)

2 medium carrots

1 large onion

Salt to taste

3 to 4 garlic cloves, peeled and left whole

Olive oil, for cooking

4 cups (1 L) chicken or vegetable stock

2 cups (500 mL) rinsed and drained canned white beans (19 oz/540 mL can)

½ cup (125 mL) whipping cream or half-and-half (optional)

¼ to ½ tsp (1 to 2.5 mL) freshly grated nutmeg

Pinch or two of cayenne pepper (optional)

⅓ to ½ cup (80 to 125 mL) vegetable oil

1 Tbsp (15 mL) finely chopped fresh parsley

SOUP THAT TASTES like autumn; it's both homey and elegant. The parsnip chips are easy to make, and really make this soup special.

Preheat the oven to 400°F.

Peel the parsnips and carrots. Shave one parsnip into strips with a vegetable peeler until you have about 1 packed cup of strips and set aside. Cut the carrots and parsnips (including the remainder of the first one) into 1-inch chunks, splitting the wide end of the parsnips into halves or quarters if they're quite large. Peel the onion, cut in half around its equator, and then cut each half into 8 chunks. Tip the vegetables onto a large rimmed baking sheet, drizzle with oil, and season lightly with salt. Toss to coat with the oil, then roast for 20 minutes, stirring halfway through. Add the garlic, stir to coat with the oil in the pan, and roast for another 15 to 25 minutes, or until everything is turning golden and tender when poked with a knife. Remove from the oven and transfer to a large saucepan. Add the stock and beans and bring to a simmer.

Cook over gentle heat until the vegetables are very tender, about 25 to 30 minutes, and then let cool. (The soup can be made ahead of time to this point and kept chilled until you're ready to proceed.) Purée the cooled soup in batches in a blender or food processor, then return to the same

saucepan. Warm the blended soup gently, and when it's completely warmed through, add the cream (if using), nutmeg (tasting as you go), and cayenne.

TO MAKE THE PARSNIP CHIPS: heat the vegetable oil in a small saucepan over medium heat until it's shimmering slightly, but not boiling. Test the oil with a piece of bread held with a pair of tongs: the bread should sizzle immediately when it touches the oil. Working in 3 to 4 batches, transfer the reserved parsnip strips to the hot oil with a fork (be sure to protect yourself from spatters from the hot oil—use an oven mitt and keep your face and torso away from the pan). Cook until very lightly browned, about 1 to 2 minutes, and then transfer to a plate covered in a double thickness of paper towels to drain. Set the parsnip chips aside until the soup is ready to serve. (If you want to make the chips more than 2 hours ahead of time, just transfer the cooled chips to an airtight container and reheat in the oven for a few minutes to crisp them up again.)

Serve the soup warm, topped with a portion of the parsnip chips and a little finely chopped parsley.

# ROASTED TOMATO SOUP
## with Red Lentils & Steel-Cut Oats
### SERVES 6 TO 8.

**SOUP:**

2 cans (28 oz/796 mL each)
  whole tomatoes
Olive oil, for cooking
1 Tbsp (15 mL) brown sugar
6 garlic cloves, peeled
2 onions, chopped
8 cups (2 L) chicken
  or vegetable stock
¼ cup (60 mL) tomato paste

3 Tbsp (45 mL) finely chopped
  sun-dried tomatoes
  (oil-packed)
1 cup (250 mL) dry red lentils
1 tsp (5 mL) dried thyme
1 tsp (5 mL) dried rosemary
⅓ cup (80 mL) steel-cut oats

**GARLIC PARMESAN CROU-
TONS (OPTIONAL):**

4 to 6 slices rustic bread
  such as ciabatta or focaccia,
  cut into cubes
Drizzle of olive oil
2 garlic cloves, minced
⅛ tsp (0.5 mL) crumbled
  dried thyme
Salt and pepper to taste
¼ to ½ cup (60 to 125 mL)
  grated Parmesan cheese

THERE ARE THREE different kinds of tomato in this soup. Three! The lentils and oats thicken it up, and the garlicky Parmesan croutons nestle right in far more comfortably than crumbled crackers. Green salad to start, Black Bean Brownies (page 244) to finish, and a good movie in the middle, and you've got yourself a fine winter evening. It's a great way to bring back summer when tomatoes aren't at their peak.

Preheat the oven to 425°F. Line a rimmed baking sheet with tin foil.

Drain the canned tomatoes in a colander set over a bowl and, using your hands, gently break open the whole tomatoes, allowing more juice to drain through to the bowl. Reserve the juices. Arrange the tomatoes in a single layer on the tin foil–lined baking sheet and drizzle with oil. Sprinkle with the sugar, season with a little salt and pepper, and roast for 30 minutes. Add the whole garlic cloves and continue to roast until there are some blackened edges (some areas of the pan may be quite black with juice—aren't you glad you lined it with tin foil?) and the garlic is softened, about 10 to 20 minutes. Remove and cool slightly.

CONTINUED . . .

CONTINUED...

In a large soup pot set over medium heat, sauté the onions in a splash of olive oil until cooked through and browned in places. Add the stock, reserved tomato juices, tomato paste, chopped dried tomatoes, lentils, and herbs. Stir well and let it come to a simmer. Coarsely smush the roasted tomatoes and garlic cloves; add to the soup. Cook for 15 minutes. Add the oats and continue cooking, stirring often, until the lentils and oats are tender, about 10 to 15 minutes. Serve hot and top with croutons just before serving.

TO MAKE THE CROUTONS: Preheat the oven to 350°F. Spread the cubes of bread over a rimmed baking sheet. Drizzle lightly with olive oil and toss around on the sheet to coat. Sprinkle the garlic, thyme, salt and pepper, and half the grated Parmesan over the bread, and bake for 5 minutes. Toss again, sprinkle with the remaining cheese, and bake until quite hard, another 10 to 15 minutes.

# SEAFOOD CHOWDER

SERVES 4 TO 6.

2 slices bacon, chopped
1 large onion, chopped
14 oz (398 mL) can clam nectar
5 oz (142 g) can baby clams, undrained
3 medium red-skinned potatoes, scrubbed and diced (peeling optional)

1 bay leaf, left whole
¼ tsp (1 mL) dried thyme
2 cups (500 mL) rinsed and drained canned white beans (19 oz/540 mL can)
1½ cups (375 mL) milk
¼ cup (60 mL) whipping cream or half-and-half

(or substitute extra milk if you prefer)
1 lb (500 g) mixed chopped fish and shellfish, thawed if frozen
Fresh parsley, chopped, for garnish (optional)

THIS RECIPE ALLOWS for a range of fish and shellfish combinations. A mixture of firm-fleshed white fish (such as halibut or snapper) with prawns and scallops works nicely, but using fish alone is fine, and more economical. For a different take, salmon can be substituted; just check that the fish has been carefully deboned. To remove skin, leave the fish in one or two pieces and cook it in the soup skin-on for a few minutes. Lift it out, and as soon as it's cool enough to handle, remove and discard the skin, then cut the fish into pieces and return it to the pot. Leftover soup is best reheated gently.

In a large saucepan set over medium heat, cook the bacon until crisp. Transfer the bacon to a plate and pour off all but 1 to 2 Tbsp of the fat. Add the onion to the saucepan and sauté until transparent and just starting to brown, 4 to 5 minutes. Return the reserved bacon to the saucepan and add the clam nectar, baby clams with their liquid, potatoes, bay leaf, and thyme. Bring to a simmer. Cook over low heat until the potatoes are cooked through, about 20 minutes.

In the meantime, purée the beans with some of the milk in a food processor or blender until completely smooth. Add the puréed beans, remaining milk, and cream (if using) to the pot once the potatoes are cooked. Bring the soup back up to a simmer, but don't allow it to boil. Add the fish (but not prawns or scallops if you're using them). Cook at a bare simmer until the fish is nearly cooked through, 4 to 6 minutes. Add the prawns and scallops and cook until the fish and shellfish are just cooked, another 4 to 6 minutes. Remove the bay leaf and serve immediately, topped with parsley if you like.

# BLACK-EYED PEA & KALE SOUP
## *with Cheesy Croutons*
### SERVES 4 TO 6.

**CROUTONS:**

1 garlic clove, crushed

¼ cup (60 mL) olive or canola oil

4 to 6 thick slices crusty French or Italian bread

¼ to ½ cup (60 to 125 mL) grated Parmesan cheese

**SOUP:**

Canola or olive oil, for cooking

1 onion or leek, finely chopped

3 to 4 garlic cloves, crushed or chopped

14 oz (398 mL) can diced or stewed tomatoes

3 cups (750 mL) chicken or vegetable stock

2 cups (500 mL) cooked black-eyed peas or white beans, or a 19 oz (540 mL) can, rinsed and drained

1 bunch kale, washed and thinly sliced (discard the ribs)

Salt and pepper to taste

WE FEEL LIKE BETTER, more virtuous people for eating a soup like this. Look at all the good stuff in it! You could easily swap any little white bean for the black-eyed peas. It tastes better the next day—if you are on the ball and plan ahead, you can prepare it up to the point of adding the kale, then cool and refrigerate overnight (or for up to two days). Reheat on the stovetop and when it's steaming, add the kale and serve.

Preheat the oven to 400°F.

TO MAKE THE CROUTONS: Put the garlic clove into a small dish with the oil and let it sit for a few minutes to infuse the oil. Place the bread on a baking sheet and brush both sides with the infused oil; bake for 10 minutes, until golden. Take the sheet out of the oven, flip the bread over, and sprinkle with cheese, then return the pan to the oven for a few minutes, until the cheese melts.

TO MAKE THE SOUP: Heat a drizzle of oil in a heavy pot set over medium-high heat. Sauté the onion for about 5 minutes, until soft. Add the garlic and cook for another minute. Add the tomatoes, stock, and beans and bring to a simmer.

Add the kale and stir; cook for a minute or two, until the kale wilts. Season with salt and pepper and serve hot, topping each bowl with a cheesy crouton.

# SAUSAGE & CHICKPEA SOUP
## *with Garlic & Avocado*
### SERVES 4.

Canola or olive oil, for cooking

½ to 1 lb (250 to 500 g) fresh chicken, turkey, or Italian sausage (1 to 3 sausages)

1 garlic bulb, cloves separated, peeled, and chopped

1 jalapeño pepper, seeded and finely chopped

1 tsp (5 mL) ground cumin

14 oz (398 mL) can diced tomatoes, undrained

2 cups (500 mL) cooked chickpeas, or a 19 oz (540 mL) can, rinsed and drained

4 cups (1 L) chicken or beef stock

Squeeze of lime juice

Salt and pepper to taste

Sour cream, for garnish (optional)

1 avocado, chopped

Fresh cilantro, for garnish (optional)

Lime wedges, for garnish (optional)

THIS SIMPLE SOUP IS amazingly flavourful, and a great way to stretch a small amount of meat to serve a larger group. The amount of garlic seems like a lot, but cooking mellows it out. For a spicier version, use chorizo or hot Italian sausage. To make it more substantial, ladle the hot soup over a scoop of quinoa, couscous, or rice.

In a large saucepan, heat a drizzle of oil over medium-high heat. Add the sausage and garlic and sauté until the sausage is golden brown and cooked through, breaking it up with a spoon. Add the jalapeño and cumin and cook for another minute or two.

Add the tomatoes and tomato juice, chickpeas, and stock and bring to a simmer. Reduce the heat to medium-low and simmer for 30 minutes, until everything is cooked through and the broth has thickened slightly. Add a squeeze of lime, season with salt and pepper, and serve hot, topped (if you like) with sour cream, chopped avocado, and fresh cilantro, with extra lime wedges served alongside.

# CHICKEN, WHITE BEAN,
## Corn & Cheddar Chowder
### SERVES 6.

3 slices bacon, chopped, or a
  drizzle of canola or olive oil
  and a pat of butter
1 large onion, finely chopped
1 celery stalk, chopped
2 Tbsp (30 mL) all-purpose
  flour
1 tsp (5 mL) ground cumin
  or thyme

4 cups (1 L) chicken stock
1 to 2 small thin-skinned
  potatoes, diced (peeling
  optional)
2 cups (500 mL) cooked white
  beans, or a 19 oz (540 mL)
  can, rinsed and drained
12 oz (341 mL) can kernel corn,
  or kernels scraped from
  2 corn cobs

1 cup (250 mL) chopped
  cooked chicken
½ cup (125 mL) half-and-half
  or whipping cream
1 cup (250 mL) shredded old
  cheddar cheese
Salt and pepper to taste

THIS HEARTY CHOW-der is perfect to make with the meaty stock you get from simmering a leftover chicken carcass—if there's still meat clinging to the bones, it will fall off into the stock, and you won't need to add any extra.

In a large saucepan set over medium-high heat, cook the bacon (if using) until crisp. Transfer it to paper towels to drain and cool, then crumble and set it aside. If you're not using bacon, heat a drizzle of oil and blob of butter in the saucepan over medium heat.

Sauté the onion and celery in the bacon drippings (or oil and butter) for about 5 minutes, until soft. Add the flour and cumin and cook, stirring, for another minute. Stir in the stock, potatoes, and beans and bring to a simmer. Reduce the heat, cover, and cook for about 10 minutes, until the potatoes are tender.

Stir in the corn, chicken, and cream and allow the chowder to return to a gentle simmer. Add the cheese and stir just until it melts. Season with salt and pepper and serve hot, topped with the crumbled bacon, if using.

# CHORIZO, BLACK BEAN
## *& Corn Chowder*
### SERVES 6.

Canola or olive oil, for cooking
1 onion, chopped
1 carrot, peeled and chopped
1 celery stalk, chopped
1 to 2 fresh chorizo or Italian
  sausages, or about ¼ lb
  (125 g) ground turkey
2 to 3 green onions, chopped
2 to 3 garlic cloves, crushed

½ tsp (2.5 mL) ground cumin
1 to 2 cups (250 to 500 mL)
  corn kernels (fresh, scraped
  off the cob, frozen, or
  canned)
1 cup (250 mL) cooked
  black beans, or half a 19 oz
  (540 mL) can, rinsed
  and drained

1 Yukon Gold or red potato,
  diced (or a handful of baby
  new potatoes, halved)
4 cups (1 L) chicken stock
½ to 1 cup (125 to 250 mL)
  half-and-half, or one 14 oz
  (398 mL) can coconut milk

THIS WAS ONE OF OUR favourite soups—we loved it even in the midst of recipe testing, when we were eating beans for breakfast, lunch, and dinner. We didn't pawn any of this stuff off on the neighbours. The chorizo adds a ton of flavour to the soup; it's a great way to stretch a small amount of flavourful meat a long way.

In a large saucepan set over medium-high heat, heat a drizzle of oil and sauté the onion, carrot, and celery for about 5 minutes, until soft. Add the chorizo sausage, squeezed out of its casing, and cook, breaking it up with a spoon, until the meat is no longer pink. Stir in the green onions, garlic, and cumin and cook for another minute or two.

Add the corn, beans, potato, and stock and bring to a simmer. Reduce the heat, cover, and cook for about 20 minutes, until the potatoes are tender. Simmer for a bit longer (uncovered) if you'd like it to thicken up a bit, then stir in the cream or coconut milk and heat through. Serve immediately.

# CURRIED SWEET POTATO,
## *Carrot & Red Lentil Soup*
### SERVES 6.

Canola or olive oil, for cooking
1 onion, chopped
1 to 2 garlic cloves, crushed
1 Tbsp (15 mL) grated
   fresh ginger
½ cup (125 mL) dry red lentils

1 medium sweet potato, peeled
   and cut into chunks
1 carrot, peeled and chopped
2 tsp (10 mL) curry paste
   or powder
4 cups (1 L) chicken
   or vegetable stock

Salt to taste
½ to 1 cup (125 to 250 mL)
   half-and-half (optional)
Plain yogurt or sour cream,
   for serving (optional)

THIS IS ONE OF THE most popular soups in our houses—many a yogurt containerful can be found in both of our freezers. (Fortunately it's easily identifiable by virtue of being bright orange.) If you don't want to use cream, swirl in some plain yogurt or evaporated milk at the end, or leave it out altogether. We have been known to take this soup with us in our to-go coffee cups to sip on in the car or at our desks. One can only drink so much coffee (trust us on that).

In a large saucepan, heat a drizzle of oil over medium-high heat. Sauté the onion, garlic, and ginger for about 5 minutes, until the onion is soft. Add the lentils, sweet potato, carrot, curry paste, stock, and salt, along with a cup of water. Bring to a boil, then turn the heat down, cover, and simmer for 30 minutes or so, until the vegetables are very tender.

Add the cream, if you're using it, and use a handheld immersion blender to purée the soup right in the pot. Taste and adjust seasonings if needed. Serve immediately or cool and refrigerate to reheat when you want it. Serve hot, with a dollop of yogurt or sour cream, if you like.

**NOTE:**
For a delicious variation, replace the sweet potato with butternut squash and the carrot with an apple or pear.

# ROASTED RED PEPPER, TOMATO
## & Black Bean Soup
### SERVES 6.

4 to 5 large, ripe tomatoes
1 red, yellow, or orange bell
  pepper, seeded and halved
3 to 5 garlic cloves, peeled
1 jalapeño pepper, seeded and
  halved (optional)
Canola or olive oil, for cooking
1 onion, chopped

1 celery stalk, chopped
1 tsp (5 mL) ground cumin
4 cups (1 L) chicken or
  vegetable stock
Salt and pepper to taste
1½ cups (375 mL) cooked black
  beans, or a 14 oz (398 mL)
  can, rinsed and drained

½ cup (125 mL) half-and-half
  (optional)

Steamed rice, for serving
  (optional)
Crumbled feta, for serving
  (optional)

ROASTING TOMATOES and peppers intensifies their flavours, caramelizing their natural sugars and creating a wonderfully intense tomato soup.

Preheat the oven to 400°F. Line a rimmed baking sheet with tin foil. Place the tomatoes, peppers, garlic, and jalapeño on the sheet. Drizzle with oil and toss to coat the veggies. Arrange them cut side down in a single layer. Roast for about 30 minutes, until the vegetables are soft and the skin of the peppers is blistered. Remove from the oven. When the peppers are cool enough to handle, peel off their skin.

Meanwhile, in a large soup pot, heat a drizzle of oil over medium-high heat and sauté the onion and celery for 5 minutes, until soft. Add the cumin and cook for another minute. Scrape the roasted tomatoes and peppers into the pot, including any juices that have collected in the bottom of the pan, and add the stock. Bring to a simmer and cook for about 20 minutes, until everything is nice and soft.

Season with salt and pepper and purée with a handheld immersion blender until smooth. Stir in the black beans and cream (if using) and heat through. If you like, pile some rice and/or feta in the bottom of each serving bowl before ladling the hot soup overtop.

# SAUSAGE, BLACK BEAN
## & Sweet Potato Soup
### SERVES 4 TO 6.

Canola or olive oil, for cooking
1 to 2 fresh mild or hot Italian
  sausages
1 jalapeño pepper, seeded
  and minced

1 medium sweet potato, peeled
  and diced
2 cups (500 mL) cooked black
  beans, or a 19 oz (540 mL)
  can, rinsed and drained
1 tsp (5 mL) ground cumin

4 cups (1 L) chicken or
  vegetable stock
1 cup (250 mL) tomato sauce,
  or half a 5.5 oz (156 mL) can
  tomato paste
Salt and pepper to taste

ANOTHER RECIPE IN the heaviest of rotations around here. It was first constructed from the dregs of the refrigerator at the end of a summer holiday in Tofino. Now we go out of our way to make it. It really couldn't be easier. Choose the rounder, darker-fleshed sweet potatoes (often labelled "yams"), which are more nutrient-dense than the longer, paler ones. This soup is made more substantial by serving over a scoop of rice or quinoa. It's better the next day.

In a large saucepan, heat a drizzle of oil over medium-high heat. Squeeze the sausage out of its casing into the pot and cook it, breaking it up as you stir it around, until it's no longer pink. Add the jalapeño, cook for another minute or two, then add the sweet potato, beans, cumin, stock, and tomato sauce.

Bring to a simmer, reduce the heat, and simmer for about half an hour, until the potatoes are tender and the broth has thickened a bit. Season with salt and pepper.

# SPINACH, BEAN & PASTA SOUP

## SERVES 4 TO 6.

Canola or olive oil, for cooking

1 fresh hot or mild Italian or chorizo sausage (optional)

1 onion, chopped

3 garlic cloves, crushed

2 cups (500 mL) water

¾ to 1 cup (185 to 250 mL) dry fusilli or other small pasta

14 oz (398 mL) can tomato sauce (any kind of pasta sauce works well) or diced tomatoes

3 cups (750 mL) chicken or vegetable stock

1 tsp (5 mL) dried oregano or basil

Salt and pepper to taste

A few big handfuls of spinach, torn or coarsely chopped

2 cups (500 mL) cooked white or red kidney beans, or a 19 oz (540 mL) can, rinsed and drained

Freshly grated Parmesan cheese, for serving

THIS WONDERFUL, hearty soup is a meal in itself—the combination of beans and pasta produces a complete protein. Omit the sausage for an equally delicious vegetarian soup. Either way, make sure you serve it with a loaf of fresh crusty bread to mop up the broth.

In a large saucepan set over medium heat, heat a drizzle of oil and sauté the sausage, breaking it up with a spoon, until it's no longer pink. Add the onion and garlic and cook for 2 to 3 minutes, until soft.

Add the water, pasta, tomato sauce, stock, oregano, and salt and pepper. Bring to a boil, reduce the heat, and simmer for about 15 minutes, until the pasta is tender. Add the spinach and beans and cook the soup for another 3 to 5 minutes. If it seems too thick, thin it with a little extra stock, tomato juice, or water.

Ladle into bowls and top each serving with Parmesan while it's still hot.

# SAUSAGE, LENTIL & BARLEY SOUP

### SERVES 6.

⅓ cup (80 mL) dry green lentils
⅓ cup (80 mL) pearl or pot
   barley
Canola or olive oil, for cooking

1 to 2 fresh mild or hot Italian
   sausages
Half a bunch of celery (about
   5 stalks), including leaves

8 cups (2 L) chicken or
   vegetable stock or water
Salt and pepper to taste

THIS SOUP MADE headlines when it was served to Leonard Nimoy (Spock!) during his visit to the Calgary Comic Expo in 2010—he said it was delicious. A steaming bowlful of it will help you live long and prosper.

Put the lentils and barley into a small pot and fill with water so that it covers the lentils and barley by about an inch. Bring to a boil, turn the heat down, and simmer for about 40 minutes, until both are tender. Drain well and set aside.

In a large soup pot, heat a drizzle of oil over medium-high heat. Squeeze the sausage out of its casing into the pot and cook, breaking it up with a spoon, until no longer pink. Chop half a bunch of celery (we start at the leafy end and go about halfway down) and throw it in the pot. Cook, stirring, for about 5 minutes.

Add the stock and cooked lentils and barley. Turn the heat down to low and simmer for about half an hour. Season with salt and pepper and serve hot.

# CHICKEN & WHITE BEAN STEW
## with Pesto
### SERVES 6.

Canola or olive oil, for cooking
1 large onion, chopped
1 lb (500 g) skinless, boneless
    chicken thighs or breasts, cut
    into bite-sized pieces
2 celery stalks, chopped
2 carrots, peeled and chopped
1 red bell pepper, seeded and
    chopped

3 to 4 garlic cloves, crushed
½ tsp (2.5 mL) ground cumin
2 cups (500 mL) cooked white
    beans, or a 19 oz (540 mL)
    can, rinsed and drained
½ to 1 cup (125 to 250 mL)
    corn kernels (optional)
1 cup (250 mL) chicken
    or vegetable stock

A few drops of Tabasco or a
    pinch of dried red chili flakes
    (optional)
Salt and pepper to taste
¼ cup (60 mL, or a couple
    of big spoonfuls) basil or
    sun-dried tomato pesto

THIS IS A PERFECT example of a potful of perfectly ordinary ingredients that is far better than the sum of its parts. The recipe is as straightforward as any, but the soup is surprisingly rich and tasty. The longer you simmer it, the better it gets—and of course it's even better the next day. It also makes great use of leftover roast turkey.

In a large pot set over medium heat, drizzle in some oil and sauté the onion for about 5 minutes, until soft. Add the chicken and cook until it's opaque. Add the celery, carrots, and red pepper and cook for a few more minutes, until the vegetables begin to soften. Add the garlic and cumin and cook for another minute.

Add the beans, corn (if using), chicken stock, Tabasco, and salt and pepper, and bring to a simmer. Turn the heat down to low, cover, and cook for about an hour, until thickened and stewlike.

Stir in the pesto and serve warm, or cool and refrigerate overnight, and reheat when you need it.

# WHITE BEAN VICHYSSOISE
## (Potato & Leek Soup)
### SERVES 4 TO 6.

2 medium leeks
Canola or olive oil, for cooking
1 Tbsp (15 mL) butter
1 small onion, chopped
2 to 4 garlic cloves, crushed

1 lb (500 g) potatoes (russet
 or Yukon Gold), peeled and
 chopped
2 cups (500 mL) cooked white
 beans, or a 19 oz (540 mL)
 can, rinsed and drained

4 cups (1 L) chicken stock
Salt and pepper to taste
½ cup (125 mL) half-and-half
 or whipping cream
Thyme for garnish (optional)

THERE ARE FEW FOODS more consoling than soup and potatoes. Leek and potato soup gets a fancy name, vichyssoise, when it's served chilled—but we like to call it by its fancy name even when it's hot. If you have some fresh tarragon kicking around, it goes very well in this, too.

Cut the leeks in half lengthwise before you wash them—sand and grit tend to work their way in between the layers, so wash them thoroughly. Thinly slice the white and pale green parts crosswise and throw out the green tops.

Drizzle some oil into a soup pot set over medium-high heat, and add the butter. When the foam subsides, sauté the leeks, onion, and garlic for about 8 minutes, until soft and translucent. Add the potatoes, beans, and stock and bring to a boil. Reduce the heat and simmer for about 30 minutes, until the potatoes are very tender.

Purée the soup in a blender or food processor, or use a handheld immersion blender right in the pot. Season with salt and pepper and stir in the cream.

Serve hot, at room temperature, or put it in the refrigerator and serve it chilled. Garnish with thyme before serving.

One-Dish Meals

# CHANA MASALA

SERVES 6.

Canola or olive oil, for cooking

1 onion, chopped

1 jalapeño or other small chili pepper, seeded and chopped

3 to 4 garlic cloves, crushed or chopped

1 Tbsp (15 mL) grated fresh ginger

1 tsp (5 mL) paprika

1 tsp (5 mL) ground cumin

½ tsp (2.5 mL) ground coriander

½ tsp (2.5 mL) garam masala

½ tsp (2.5 mL) salt

¼ tsp (1 mL) turmeric

3 tomatoes, chopped

¼ cup (60 mL) chopped fresh cilantro (stems too)

1 cup (250 mL) chicken, vegetable, or beef stock or water

4 cups (1 L) cooked chickpeas, or two 19 oz (540 mL) cans, rinsed and drained

Steamed rice or couscous, for serving

Extra cilantro, for serving (optional—leave out the stems this time)

THIS SPICED CHICKPEA bliss (classic use of a legume, right here) is one of our favourite lunches to eat at our desks. The ingredient list seems daunting, but it's really a snap to pull together. It gets better with a day or two to hang out in the refrigerator, so it's the perfect thing to make a big batch of to dip into all week. Make a big pot of brown rice, too—it keeps just as well. If you like your chana masala spicy, add another jalapeño or small chili to bump up the heat.

Drizzle a generous amount of oil into a large, heavy skillet set over medium-high heat. Sauté the onion for a few minutes, until soft; add the jalapeño, garlic, and ginger and cook for another few minutes, until everything is soft and fragrant. Add the paprika, cumin, coriander, garam masala, salt, and turmeric and cook for another minute. Add the tomatoes and cilantro and cook for about 5 minutes, breaking up the tomatoes with a spoon. Add a little of the water or stock if the pan is too dry.

When the tomatoes are breaking apart, add the stock and chickpeas, bring to a simmer, turn the heat down low, and cover. Cook for about 30 minutes, until everything is nice and soft and the sauce has thickened. Serve immediately over rice, scattered with extra cilantro, or cool and refrigerate for a day or two to give the flavours a chance to get to know each other, then reheat.

# RED LENTIL
## & Sweet Potato Curry with Spinach
SERVES 4 TO 6.

Canola or olive oil, for cooking

1 onion, chopped

1 jalapeño pepper, seeded and finely chopped

1 Tbsp (15 mL) grated fresh ginger

3 garlic cloves, crushed

2 tsp (10 mL) curry paste or powder

1 tsp (5 mL) ground cumin

1 tsp (5 mL) turmeric

½ tsp (2.5 mL) salt

1 medium dark-fleshed sweet potato, peeled and cut into ½-inch chunks

½ cup (125 mL) dry red lentils

14 oz (398 mL) can coconut milk

1 cup (250 mL) water

1 cup (250 mL) packed baby spinach leaves

Steamed rice, for serving

THIS CURRY BRINGS out the best in everyone at the party (meaning everything in the pan); as a result, it's now in heavy rotation in both of our households.

In a large, heavy skillet, heat a drizzle of oil over medium-high heat. Sauté the onion for about 5 minutes, until soft; add the jalapeño, ginger, garlic, curry paste, cumin, turmeric, and salt. Cook for a few more minutes.

Stir in the sweet potato, lentils, coconut milk, and water; bring to a simmer, then cover, turn the heat down to medium-low, and cook for about 20 minutes, until the potato is tender.

Uncover the skillet and tear in the spinach; stir, replace the lid, and cook for another minute or two, just until the spinach wilts. Serve immediately, over rice.

One-Dish Meals

# QUICK CHICKPEA CURRY

### SERVES 4.

Canola or olive oil, for cooking

1 tsp (5 mL) cumin seeds (or add ground cumin along with the curry paste)

1 small onion, chopped

1 jalapeño pepper, seeded and finely chopped (optional)

2 Tbsp (30 mL) chopped fresh cilantro (finely chopped stems are fine too)

1 Tbsp (15 mL) grated fresh ginger

1 to 2 tsp (5 to 10 mL) curry paste or powder

1 to 2 tomatoes, or a few canned tomatoes, coarsely chopped

2 cups (500 mL) cooked chickpeas, or a 19 oz (540 mL) can, rinsed and drained

Half to a full 14 oz (398 mL) can coconut milk (regular or light)

1 tsp (5 mL) salt

CHICKPEAS (ALL legumes, really—don't mean to play favourites) are the ultimate fast, healthy convenience food. They'll hang out forever on your pantry shelf, waiting to be turned into something like this in under 10 minutes.

In a large skillet, heat a glug of oil over medium-high heat. Add the cumin seed and cook for a minute or two, until fragrant. Add the onion and cook for 5 minutes, until soft and starting to turn golden. Add the jalapeño, cilantro, ginger, and curry paste and cook for another minute, then add the tomatoes, chickpeas, half the can of coconut milk, and salt. Bring to a simmer, cover, and cook for 5 to 8 minutes, until everything softens and thickens. If it's too thick, or if you like it saucier, add more coconut milk. Taste and adjust seasoning, then serve hot, over rice.

# ALOO GOBI WITH CHICKPEAS

## SERVES 4 TO 6.

Canola or olive oil, for cooking

1 medium head cauliflower, separated into florets

1 onion, finely chopped

1 Tbsp (15 mL) grated fresh ginger

1 Tbsp (15 mL) garam masala

2 tsp (10 mL) ground cumin, or 1 Tbsp (15 mL) cumin seeds

2 tsp (10 mL) chili powder

½ tsp (2.5 mL) salt

2 to 3 tomatoes, chopped

1 smallish sweet potato, peeled and diced, or 2 thin-skinned

white potatoes, diced (about 3 cups/750 mL)

2 cups (500 mL) cooked chickpeas or red kidney beans, or a 19 oz (540 mL) can, rinsed and drained

ALOO (POTATOES) gobi (cauliflower) is a potato-cauliflower curry; this version incorporates beans and uses sweet potatoes for a flavour and nutrition boost. The tomatoes melt around the sweet potatoes, mingling with the spices and creating a sticky-sweet, smoky almost-sauce.

Preheat the oven to 425°F.

Spread the cauliflower out in a single layer on a rimmed baking sheet; drizzle with oil and toss around with your hands to coat the pieces. Roast for 20 minutes, until tender and starting to turn golden on the bottoms and edges.

Meanwhile, heat a generous drizzle of oil in a large, heavy skillet. Add the onion and cook for a few minutes, until starting to soften. Add the ginger, garam masala, cumin, chili powder, and salt and cook for a minute, then add the tomatoes, sweet potato, and chickpeas or kidney beans. Stir to combine everything well, pour 1 cup (250 mL) water overtop, and cover with a lid; reduce the heat to medium-low and cook for 8 to 10 minutes, until the sweet potato is tender.

Add the roasted cauliflower to the pan and stir to combine everything well, adding a little more water if it seems too dry, and seasoning with salt if needed.

# VEGETABLE LENTIL CURRY
## SERVES 4 TO 6 (DEPENDING ON WHAT YOU ADD).

Canola or olive oil, for cooking

1 onion, peeled and thinly sliced or chopped

2 garlic cloves, crushed

1 Tbsp (15 mL) grated fresh ginger (bottled is OK, unlike bottled garlic)

1 to 2 tsp (5 to 10 mL) curry paste

1 red, orange, or yellow bell pepper, chopped

1 to 2 cups (250 to 500 mL) zucchini, green beans, potatoes, cauliflower, or eggplant, chopped into bite-sized pieces

14 oz (398 mL) can diced tomatoes, drained, or 1 or 2 fresh tomatoes, chopped

1 cup (250 mL) cooked green lentils, or half a 19 oz (540 mL) can, rinsed and drained

14 oz (398 mL) can coconut milk

¼ cup (60 mL) mango or peach chutney (optional)

1 small tart apple, cored and chopped, or a handful of golden raisins

Salt and pepper to taste

1 cup (250 mL) packed fresh spinach, torn or chopped

Chopped peanuts or cashews, to sprinkle on top (optional)

A CURRY MAKES GREAT use of canned ingredients (you have lentils, tomatoes, and coconut milk in your pantry, right?) and whatever veg are in season. Use any vegetables you like or need to get rid of, in whatever amounts you like—just use common sense and start the sturdier veg (e.g., potatoes) earlier than the softer ones (e.g., zucchini and spinach).

In a large skillet set over medium-high heat, drizzle a bit of oil and sauté the onion for 2 to 3 minutes, until soft. Add the garlic and ginger and cook for another minute. Add the curry paste along with any veg that take longer to cook (e.g., potatoes and cauliflower) and cook for a few more minutes.

Add the bell pepper and any other veggies you like. Sauté them for a few minutes, just until they start to release their juices and soften.

Add the tomatoes and cook until most of the moisture has cooked off, then add the coconut milk and chutney and bring the mixture to a simmer. Add the apple or raisins and cook for about 5 minutes.

Season with salt and pepper and stir in the spinach; cook for a minute, just until it wilts. Serve immediately over rice, sprinkled with chopped peanuts.

# COCONUT DAL CURRY

SERVES 4 TO 6.

1½ cups (375 mL) dry red
lentils
Canola oil, for cooking
1 large onion, chopped
2 large tomatoes, chopped
2 to 3 garlic cloves, crushed

1 tsp (5 mL) curry paste
or powder
1 tsp (5 mL) sugar
½ tsp (2.5 mL) chili powder
½ tsp (2.5 mL) salt

one 14 oz (398 mL) can
coconut milk
1 tsp (5 mL) garam masala
(optional)
Handful of chopped fresh
cilantro (optional)

IN INDIA, THE TERM dal refers to around 60 varieties of dry pulses—in North America, it most often refers to a curried dish made out of them with tomatoes, garlic, and spices. It's great served with rice or naan, or alongside other curried dishes.

Put the lentils in a medium saucepan, cover with water by an inch or so, bring to a boil, and simmer for 15 to 20 minutes, until soft. Drain. Meanwhile, heat a good drizzle of oil in a separate saucepan and sauté the onion for 7 to 8 minutes, until golden. Add the tomatoes and garlic and cook for another 5 minutes. Add the curry paste, sugar, chili powder, and salt, then the cooked lentils, and cook for another 5 minutes. Add the coconut milk and cook until it has the consistency you want—dal can be runny but will thicken up as you continue to cook it.

Remove from the heat and stir in the garam masala, then sprinkle with cilantro, if you like. Serve immediately—as is, or with rice or naan.

# COUSCOUS
## *with Roasted Vegetables, Feta & Chickpeas*
SERVES 4 TO 6, DEPENDING ON WHAT YOU PUT INTO IT AND WHETHER
IT'S SERVED AS A SIDE OR THE MAIN EVENT.

| | | |
|---|---|---|
| 1 small sweet potato, peeled and cut into chunks | 1 garlic bulb, separated into cloves and peeled | Salt and pepper to taste |
| 1 red or yellow bell pepper, seeded and chopped | 2 cups (500 mL) rinsed and drained canned chickpeas (19 oz/540 mL can) | 1 cup (250 mL) couscous, regular or whole wheat |
| 1 zucchini, halved lengthwise and thickly sliced | Canola or olive oil, for roasting | ½ to 1 cup (125 to 250 mL) crumbled feta cheese |

WE LISTED ingredients only because you kind of have to in order to print a recipe; really, you can chop any number of vegetables into coarse chunks—who cares if they are of varying size, and you get some softer pieces and some blackened bits—and roast them until they're soft and crispy-edged. Try sweet potatoes, squash, beets, red peppers, zucchini, asparagus . . . whatever you like or is in season. Try swapping other grains—rice, quinoa, and barley all work well—for the couscous, which is actually little bits of pasta.

Preheat the oven to 450°F.

Spread the vegetables, garlic, and chickpeas on a large rimmed baking sheet. Drizzle with oil, sprinkle with salt and pepper, and toss with your hands to coat everything with oil. Spread out into a single layer.

Roast for 20 to 30 minutes, tossing when you think of it, until the vegetables are done to your liking. Meanwhile, put the couscous into a medium bowl and pour 1¼ cups boiling water overtop; cover with a plate and let sit for 5 to 10 minutes.

Fluff the steamed couscous with a fork and scrape the roasted veg into the bowl, along with the feta. Serve immediately, while still warm.

# LENTIL & MUSHROOM BOURGUIGNON

### SERVES 4 TO 6.

Canola or olive oil, for cooking

1 small yellow or purple onion, finely chopped

2 Tbsp (30 mL) butter

3 garlic cloves, crushed

2 large portobello mushrooms, sliced (discard the stems and scrape out the gills)

2 to 3 cups (500 to 750 mL) sliced button, brown, or cremini mushrooms (or a combination)

½ cup (125 mL) cooked or canned brown lentils, rinsed and drained

1 cup (250 mL) red wine

1 Tbsp (15 mL) all-purpose flour

2 to 3 cups (500 to 750 mL) beef, onion, or vegetable stock

1 Tbsp (15 mL) tomato paste (optional)

1 to 2 cups (250 to 500 mL) pearl onions, peeled

Egg noodles or mashed potatoes, for serving

THIS BOURGUIGNON was one of our first triumphs. Carnivorous husbands loved it. Preschoolers thought the slabs of portobello mushrooms were meat. It was rich and hearty and meaty (yet meatless) and went very well with a bottle of red. (Not for the preschoolers!) The tomato paste enriches it, but the night we ran out it was still perfectly edible. If you're cooking with a friend, peeling those wee onions is far more fun—they really are worth the effort.

In a large, heavy skillet, heat a drizzle of oil and sauté the onion for 2 to 3 minutes, until soft. Add the butter, garlic, and mushrooms and cook until the mushrooms release their liquid, soften, and then start to brown—add another drizzle of oil if the pan seems too dry.

Add the lentils and cook for 1 or 2 minutes, then add the wine and cook for a few minutes more, scraping any browned bits off the bottom of the skillet, until the wine has almost cooked off. Sprinkle the flour overtop and stir to blend, then add the beef stock and tomato paste. Bring to a simmer and cook, stirring often, for about 10 minutes, or until the sauce is thick and dark and the mushrooms are tender. If the sauce is too thick, add a little more stock.

Meanwhile, heat a drizzle of oil in a small skillet (add a dab of butter, too, if you like) and cook the pearl onions over medium-high heat until golden and soft; add to the mushroom mixture. Serve hot, over buttered egg noodles or mashed potatoes.

# ROASTED SAUSAGES
## *with Braised Lentils*
### SERVES 4 TO 6.

Olive or canola oil, for cooking

4 to 6 large fresh sausages (chicken, lamb, and Italian all work well)

1 red or yellow onion, finely chopped

1 carrot, finely chopped

1 stalk celery, finely chopped

2 garlic cloves, crushed

1 cup (250 mL) dry green lentils

3 cups (750 mL) chicken, beef, or vegetable stock

THE JUICES FROM THE sausage make the lentils über-flavourful; if you like, add a splash of red wine along with the stock.

Preheat the oven to 350°F.

Heat a drizzle of oil in a heavy skillet set over medium-high heat and brown the sausages (don't worry about cooking them through), setting aside on a plate once browned.

Add a little more oil to the skillet and sauté the onion, carrot, and celery for 3 to 4 minutes, until softened. Add the garlic and cook for another minute. Add the lentils and stock and bring to a simmer. Nestle the sausages back into the lentils and slide the skillet into the oven, then cook for 40 to 45 minutes, until the sausages are cooked through and the lentils are soft.

# PULLED PORK & BEANS

## SERVES 6.

Canola or olive oil, for cooking
(optional)

1 to 2 lb (500 g to 1 kg) pork
shoulder, country-style ribs,
or tenderloin

2 cups (500 mL) cooked red
kidney beans, or a 19 oz
(540 mL) can, rinsed and
drained

2 cups (500 mL) cooked white
kidney beans, or a 19 oz

(540 mL) can, rinsed
and drained

½ cup (125 mL) ketchup
(or half ketchup, half bottled
chili sauce)

¼ cup (60 mL) honey or
maple syrup

¼ cup (60 mL) red wine
vinegar, apple cider vinegar,
or balsamic vinegar

2 Tbsp (30 mL) brown sugar

1 Tbsp (15 mL) soy sauce

1 Tbsp (15 mL) grainy or yellow
mustard

2 to 3 garlic cloves, crushed

A few shots of Tabasco
(optional)

¼ cup (60 mL) barbecue sauce,
or to taste (optional)

PORK AND BEANS ARE such a natural pairing—we've always wondered why the pork element is limited to a teeny bit of fat per can of beans. We've righted that wrong. Pulled Pork and Beans is great served on soft buns, topped with creamy coleslaw, like traditional pulled pork. It's a little sloppier, though—we like to treat it more like sloppy joes, served warm on soft buns or slabs of cheese bread. It's also pretty fab over a baked potato, topped with cheese or not. Or, of course, you could always eat it straight up.

If you want to boost flavour in the finished dish, heat a drizzle of oil in a heavy skillet set over medium-high heat and brown the meat on all sides before transferring it to a slow cooker or baking dish. Add the remaining ingredients (except the barbecue sauce), cover, and cook on low for 6 to 8 hours (in a slow cooker), or in a 300°F oven for 4 to 4½ hours, until the pork falls apart when you poke it with a fork.

Skim as much fat as you can off the surface and pull the pork apart, right in with the beans, using 2 forks. Take out any bones, if you used bone-in pork. Stir in the barbecue sauce, if you like. Serve straight up, over rice, or sloppy joe–style on soft buns or slabs of cheese bread.

One-Dish Meals

# BEEF & BARLEY CHILI

## SERVES 10.

Canola or olive oil, for cooking

1 lb (500 g) lean ground beef or bison

1 large onion, chopped

1 small red or yellow bell pepper, seeded and chopped

3 to 4 garlic cloves, crushed

28 oz (796 mL) can diced or stewed tomatoes

2 cups (500 mL) cooked red kidney beans, or a 19 oz (540 mL) can, rinsed and drained

14 oz (398 mL) can baked beans

1 cup (250 mL) salsa

1 cup (250 mL) beef, chicken, or vegetable stock, or tomato juice

⅓ cup (80 mL) dry pearl or pot barley

2 Tbsp (30 mL) chili powder

1 Tbsp (15 mL) unsweetened cocoa powder (optional)

Salt and pepper to taste

COCOA IS THE SECRET ingredient for many chili cooks who want to make their chili deeper, darker, and richer—it won't make it taste like chocolate, but it will make it more intense. Chili is always better the next day—let it simmer when you're home, or toss everything into a slow cooker to simmer itself while you're out. To make individual bread bowls, slice the tops off dinner rolls, hollow them out, and fill with chili. (Yeah, it's gimmicky.)

In a large pot, heat a drizzle of oil over medium-high heat. Cook the beef and onion for 5 to 8 minutes, breaking the beef up with a spoon, until the onion is soft and the meat is no longer pink. Add the bell pepper and garlic and cook for a few more minutes, until the pepper is soft.

Add the tomatoes, beans, salsa, stock, barley, chili powder, cocoa, and salt and pepper and bring to a boil. Turn the heat down to low, cover, and cook for about an hour, stirring occasionally, until the chili is thick; if it's too thick, add a little more stock or tomatoes. If it's too watery, continue to cook down until it's as thick as you like. Serve immediately, or cool completely and refrigerate for a day or two, reheating when you're ready for it.

# TWO-BEAN & SWEET POTATO
## *Chipotle Chili*
### SERVES 6.

Canola or olive oil, for cooking

1 onion, chopped

1 red bell pepper, seeded and chopped

3 to 4 garlic cloves, crushed or chopped

1 medium sweet potato, peeled and cut into ½-inch pieces

28 oz (796 mL) can diced, whole, or stewed tomatoes

2 cups (500 mL) cooked black beans, or a 19 oz (540 mL) can, rinsed and drained

2 cups (500 mL) cooked red kidney beans, or a 19 oz (540 mL) can, rinsed and drained

10 oz (284 mL) can beef, onion, or vegetable broth (undiluted), or 1 bottle stout (such as Guinness)

1 Tbsp (15 mL) chili powder

1 Tbsp (15 mL) brown sugar or maple syrup

1 Tbsp (15 mL) chopped canned chipotle chile in adobo (optional)

2 tsp (10 mL) ground cumin

½ tsp (2.5 mL) salt

IF YOU LIKE, SWAP butternut squash for the sweet potato. There's no need to chop or process the canned tomatoes; even if you use whole ones, the simmering process will break them up as they cook. Chili is always better the next day; if you simmer this one afternoon (it works well in the slow cooker, too), then cool and pop it in the refrigerator over-night, dinner will already be done the next day.

In a large, heavy pot, heat a drizzle of oil over medium-high heat. Sauté the onion and red pepper for about 5 minutes, until soft. Add the garlic and cook for another minute or two. Add the sweet potato, tomatoes, beans, broth, chili powder, brown sugar, chipotle (if using), cumin, and salt and bring to a simmer.

Turn the heat to low, cover, and let simmer for about 30 minutes. Serve immediately or cool completely and refrigerate overnight, then reheat the next day.

# MEXICAN FRIED RICE

## SERVES 6.

Canola or olive oil, for cooking
½ lb (250 g) chorizo sausage, ground bison, or ground turkey
1 onion, chopped
1 jalapeño pepper, seeded and diced (optional)
1 Tbsp (15 mL) chili powder

1 tsp (5 mL) ground cumin
Pinch of salt
3 cups (750 mL) cooked rice, white or brown
2 cups (500 mL) cooked black, red kidney, or pinto beans, or a 19 oz (540 mL) can, rinsed and drained

1 tomato, seeded and chopped
½ cup (125 mL) crumbled feta or shredded old cheddar cheese (optional)
Chopped fresh cilantro, for garnish (optional)

COLD LEFTOVER RICE is best for fried rice skillets, because the grains are more separate and won't glom together in the pan—it's a good reason to double the amount of rice next time you cook a batch. To be honest, neither of us were too enamored with the idea of a Mexican-flavoured rice skillet until we tried it. It's really good. It's quick. You can toss leftovers into it—bits of chicken, pork, or shrimp, or cooked veg that are too boring to reheat on their own. It's a meal in a bowl.

In a large, heavy skillet, heat a drizzle of oil and cook the sausage (or other meat) and onion, breaking up the sausage until it's no longer pink. Once the onion is soft, add the jalapeño, chili powder, cumin, and salt and cook for another minute or two.

Remove the meat mixture from the pan and set aside. Add another drizzle of oil and the rice to the skillet; cook for a few minutes, stirring, until the rice starts to brown. Add the beans and cook for a few minutes, then add the meat mixture back into the pan along with the tomato and feta, and stir until heated through.

Divide among wide, shallow bowls and top with chopped fresh cilantro.

One-Dish Meals

# JAMAICAN RED BEANS & RICE

## SERVES 4 TO 6.

Canola or olive oil, for cooking

1 onion, chopped

2 celery stalks, chopped

1 red or yellow bell pepper, seeded and chopped

3 to 4 garlic cloves, crushed or chopped

4 cups (1 L) cooked red kidney beans, or two 19 oz (540 mL) cans, drained

4 to 5 plum tomatoes, chopped, or one 14 oz (398 mL) can diced or stewed tomatoes

¼ cup (60 mL) Pickapeppa sauce (about half a bottle)

Steamed rice, for serving

JAMAICAN RED BEANS and rice is one of the best-known beans-and-rice dishes. Pickapeppa sauce is a Jamaican condiment made with tomatoes, onions, sugar, vinegar, mangoes, raisins, tamarind, peppers, and spices—you'll find it alongside the ketchup, HP, and Worcestershire on most supermarket shelves. It's well worth seeking out if you plan to make a batch or two of red beans and rice. If you like, use half red kidney beans, half black beans.

Heat a drizzle of oil in a large saucepan set over medium heat. Add the onion, celery, red pepper, and garlic and sauté for about 10 minutes, until the onion starts to turn golden. Add the beans, tomatoes, and Pickapeppa sauce and bring to a simmer. Turn the heat down, cover, and cook for about 1 hour, until nice and thick. (Add a little water, stock, or tomato juice if it's too thick.)

If you like, let the mixture cool down and refrigerate, then reheat it after a day or two. Serve hot, over rice.

# WHITE BEAN RISOTTO
## *with Sun-Dried Tomatoes, Spinach & Parmesan*
### SERVES 6.

Olive or canola oil, for cooking

1 Tbsp (15 mL) butter (plus more, if you like)

1 small onion, finely chopped

1 fresh chorizo or Italian sausage (optional)

2 cups (500 mL) arborio (short-grain) rice

6 cups (1.5 L) low-sodium chicken or vegetable stock, warmed

1 cup (250 mL) cooked white beans, or half a 19 oz (540 mL) can, rinsed and drained

2 to 3 sun-dried tomatoes packed in oil, drained and chopped (optional)

½ to 1 cup (125 to 250 mL) freshly grated Parmesan cheese

Juice of 1 lemon

1 cup (250 mL) packed fresh spinach leaves, torn or roughly chopped, and/or a small handful of fresh basil, torn or chopped

BEFORE YOU GO GETTING ALL INTIMIDATED—honestly, if you can cook oatmeal, you can make risotto. There are two directions you can take with this recipe—many more, in fact, but to go through them all would require its own book. Adding a sausage at the beginning obviously changes the flavour of the dish, making it more substantial; leaving it out results in a lighter dish with a more predominant lemon flavour.

Asparagus is fantastic, too (chop and toss it in for the last 5 minutes of cooking time), or slice a cup or two of mushrooms and sauté them along with the onion at the beginning. Shrimp are great tossed in with the spinach. Pearl or pot barley makes a mighty fine (and more substantial) risotto, too—same drill, just expect to cook it for twice as long. See what we mean? Once you get the hang of risotto, you can make it however you want.

CONTINUED . . .

CONTINUED . . .

In a medium-large saucepan, heat a drizzle of oil with the butter over medium-high heat. Sauté the onion and sausage (squeezed out of its casing), if you're using it, until the onion is soft and the sausage is no longer pink (break it up with a spoon). Add the rice and cook for a minute, just to coat the grains with the oily juices.

Add about ½ cup of stock and cook, stirring, until it's absorbed. Continue adding stock ½ to 1 cup at a time and cook, stirring (it doesn't have to be constantly, just frequently) until it absorbs the liquid. When it's all used up (it should take about 30 minutes), the grains should be soft. If they still have a crunchy core, just add a little more water or stock. Add the beans along with the last addition of stock.

When the rice is cooked and it's nice and creamy, stir in the sun-dried tomatoes, cheese, lemon juice, spinach, and, if you like, another blob of butter. Stir until the cheese melts and the spinach wilts. Serve immediately.

# POACHED EGGS
## over Warm Lentils with Bacon
### SERVES 4.

¾ cup (185 mL) dry green
  or du Puy lentils
1 garlic clove, peeled
4 slices bacon, chopped
2 leeks (white and pale
  green parts only), halved
  lengthwise and thinly sliced,

or 1 sweet onion, finely
  chopped
2 celery stalks, finely chopped
  (leafy parts too)
1 carrot, finely chopped
2 Tbsp (30 mL) red wine or
  balsamic vinegar, or to taste

1 cup (250 mL) packed baby
  spinach leaves
Salt and pepper to taste
4 to 8 eggs

THANKS AGAIN, old issues of *Gourmet*. This made it to the top of our must-make list in under a day. (Adapted from the October 2000 issue.)

In a small saucepan, cover the lentils with about twice their volume in water, add the garlic clove, bring to a simmer, and cook uncovered for about 30 minutes, or until just tender. (You can do this ahead of time and keep them in the refrigerator until you're ready for them.)

While the lentils are simmering, cook the bacon until crisp in a large, heavy skillet; use a slotted spoon to transfer the bacon to a plate, leaving the drippings in the skillet. (If you like, pour the drippings out and add a drizzle of canola or olive oil.) Add the leeks, celery, and carrot to the pan and cook, stirring often, for about 5 minutes. Drain the lentils well and add them to the skillet along with the vinegar; cook, stirring, until heated through. Add the spinach and cook until it wilts. Season with salt and pepper and stir in the bacon.

Meanwhile, poach (or fry, if you prefer) your eggs. Divide the warm lentil salad among 4 plates and top with the eggs.

# STIR-FRIED CHICKPEAS & ASPARAGUS
## *with Brown Rice & Lemon Tahini Dressing*
### SERVES 4.

Canola or olive oil, for cooking
2 cups (500 mL) cooked
   chickpeas, or a 19 oz
   (540 mL) can, rinsed
   and drained
2 garlic cloves, crushed
1 onion, chopped

½ bunch asparagus, cut into
   1-inch pieces (about ½ lb)
2 to 3 cups (500 to 750 mL)
   cooked brown or white
   rice, or barley, cold
½ cup (125 mL) sliced or
   slivered almonds or chopped
   walnuts, toasted

**TAHINI DRESSING:**
¼ cup (60 mL) tahini (sesame
   seed paste)
Juice of 1 lemon
2 Tbsp (30 mL) canola
   or olive oil
2 Tbsp (30 mL) hot water
1 garlic clove, crushed
Pinch of salt

THIS RECIPE IS adapted from one of our favourite food blogs, *101 Cookbooks*, written by Heidi Swanson. Her combination of rice, chickpeas, and asparagus topped with tahini dressing is brilliant—typical of her recipes. We've skilleted everything separately in order to really brown and caramelize it all. This is best made with leftover rice—once cold, the grains are more separate, and won't clump together as you cook it. It's also delicious topped with a poached or fried egg. Yum.

TO MAKE THE DRESSING: shake everything up in a jar.

Heat a generous drizzle of oil in a heavy skillet set over medium-high heat; add the chickpeas and cook for a few minutes, until they start turning golden. Add the garlic and a bit of salt and cook until the chickpeas are nicely golden and getting crispy. Transfer to a shallow bowl.

Add the onion to the skillet, along with a little more oil if you need it. Cook for 4 to 5 minutes, until golden. Add the asparagus and cook for a minute or two, putting the lid on the pan if it helps, to allow the asparagus to soften a bit. Dump that into the bowl with the chickpeas.

Add another slick of oil to the skillet and cook the rice for a few minutes, just to warm it through and brown it a bit. Add the chickpeas, onion, and asparagus back to the skillet and toss it around to warm through, then divvy it up among bowls and sprinkle with the almonds. Drizzle with a bit of the tahini dressing, and pass more around at the table.

# SLOW-COOKED LAMB SHANKS
## with Lentils, Garlic & Rosemary
### SERVES 4 (OR MORE).

Olive or canola oil, for cooking
(optional)
4 lamb shanks (about
4 lb/1.8 kg total)
¾ cup (185 mL) dry green or
brown lentils

1 carrot, finely chopped
1 garlic bulb, cloves separated
and peeled
2 to 3 sprigs fresh rosemary
Salt to taste

1 cup (250 mL) red wine
(optional)
1 cup (250 mL) chicken, beef,
or vegetable stock

BROWNING THE MEAT adds flavour to the final dish—you could also brown the shanks on the barbecue first, but it isn't absolutely necessary. If you're pressed for time, just toss them straight into the slow cooker or pot. You can use this same technique with a whole leg of lamb, with or without the bone. If you do it in the slow cooker and the bone sticks out, cover the open part with tin foil to trap the heat—it works just fine! (Tip: if there are leftover lentils in a mass of sticky juices in the bottom of the pot, turn them into soup. Y.U.M.)

In a large, heavy skillet, heat a drizzle of oil over high heat and brown the lamb shanks a couple at a time, turning to brown them on all sides. (Don't worry about cooking them through.) Put the lentils and carrot in the bottom of a slow cooker or large ovenproof pot and put the browned shanks on top. Scatter with the garlic, rosemary, and a sprinkling of salt. Pour the wine and stock overtop.

Cover and cook on low for 6 to 8 hours, or bake in a 325°F oven for 3 to 3½ hours, until the lamb is very tender. Serve the shanks alongside the lentils, with roasted or boiled potatoes, or White Bean Mashed Potatoes (page 203).

One-Dish Meals

# THAI CHICKEN THIGHS
## *with Black Beans & Sweet Potatoes*
### SERVES 6.

1 to 2 lb (500 g to 1 kg) skinless chicken thighs

1 smallish dark-fleshed sweet potato, peeled and cut into chunks

1 small red bell pepper, chopped

2 cups (500 mL) cooked black beans, or a 19 oz (540 mL) can, rinsed and drained

3 to 4 garlic cloves, crushed

1 cup (250 mL) salsa

½ cup (125 mL) chicken stock or water

¼ cup (60 mL) peanut butter

2 Tbsp (30 mL) chopped fresh cilantro (optional)

1 tsp (5 mL) ground cumin

Chopped salted peanuts and/ or fresh cilantro, for garnish (optional)

Steamed rice, for serving

SLOW COOKERS ARE da bomb. You can toss ingredients in while everyone scrambles to eat breakfast, and by dinner-time you have a hot meal all ready to go. A slow cooker is to busy people what capes and leotards are to superheroes. (Maybe that's a tad dramatic.)

Put everything into a slow cooker, cover, and cook on low for 6 hours, stirring once or twice. If you don't have a slow cooker, toss everything in a pot, cover it, and bake in a 350°F oven for about 1½ hours, stirring once or twice, until the chicken is cooked through.

Serve hot over rice, garnished if you like with chopped peanuts or additional fresh cilantro.

# LAMB & LENTIL SHEPHERD'S PIE
## *with White Bean Mashed Potatoes*
### SERVES 6.

Canola or olive oil, for cooking
1 onion, finely chopped
1 carrot, finely chopped
1 lb (500 g) ground lamb
1 tsp (5 mL) chopped fresh
   rosemary or thyme

10 oz (284 mL) can beef broth
   or bouillon, undiluted
1 Tbsp (15 mL) tomato paste
2 cups (500 mL) cooked lentils,
   or a 19 oz (540 mL) can,
   rinsed and drained

Salt and pepper to taste
White Bean Mashed Potatoes
   topping (see page 203)

THIS BUBBLY, comfort-in-a-dish pie delivers a double whammy of legumes—lentils along with the lamb, and white beans puréed into the potatoes. How smart are you? Oh, so smart. And a great cook, too.

Preheat the oven to 375°F.

Prepare the White Bean Mashed Potatoes and set aside.

Drizzle some oil into a large skillet set over medium-high heat and sauté the onion, carrot, lamb, and rosemary for 5 to 8 minutes, until the vegetables are soft and the lamb is cooked through.

Add the broth, tomato paste, and lentils and bring to a simmer. Season with salt and pepper and pour into a baking dish. Spread White Bean Mashed Potatoes over the filling and bake for 30 minutes, until bubbly.

# TURKEY & BLACK BEAN CHILI
## with Butternut Squash & Apples
### SERVES 6.

Canola or olive oil, for cooking
1 onion, chopped
1 carrot, peeled and chopped
1 celery stalk, chopped
3 to 4 garlic cloves, crushed
1 lb (500 g) ground turkey, or
    2 cups leftover shredded
    roast turkey or chicken
1 small butternut squash,
    peeled, seeded, and diced
    (2 to 3 cups/500 to 750 mL)

1 large tart apple, cored
    and chopped (don't bother
    peeling it)
2 Tbsp (30 mL) chili powder
1 Tbsp (15 mL) ground cumin
10 oz (284 mL) can chicken,
    beef, or vegetable broth,
    undiluted
14 oz (398 mL) can coconut
    milk, regular or light

1 cup (250 mL) cooked
    black beans, or half a 19 oz
    (540 mL) can, rinsed and
    drained
½ cup (125 mL) salsa, or 2 Tbsp
    (30 mL) tomato paste
Salt and pepper to taste
2 to 4 Tbsp (30 to 60 mL)
    chopped fresh cilantro
    (optional)

OUR FAMOUS FOODIE friend Korey Kealey inspired this chili of sorts—or is it a stew, or a curry? Although it does contain beans, it's loaded with chunks of butternut squash and apples, with a curry quality brought on by a can of coconut milk. Très fall. If you want it to be more of a curry, add more stock or a can of diced tomatoes with their juices, and a spoonful of curry paste along with the spices.

In a large pot, heat a drizzle of oil over medium-high heat and sauté the onion, carrot and celery for about 5 minutes, until soft. Add the garlic and turkey and cook, breaking up the turkey with a spoon (if you're using ground turkey, that is), until it's no longer pink.

Add the squash, apple, chili powder, and cumin and cook for a few more minutes. Add the broth, coconut milk, beans, salsa, and salt and pepper. Bring to a simmer and cook for 30 minutes, until the squash is tender and the mixture is thick. If it's not thick enough, keep cooking it until it's the consistency you like. Stir in the cilantro or serve with it scattered on top.

NOTE:
You can also make this in the slow cooker—just toss everything in (cook the turkey first) and turn it on low for 6 hours. Best potpourri ever.

# BUTTER CHICKEN & LENTILS

## SERVES 6 TO 8.

**MARINADE AND CHICKEN:**
1½ tsp (7.5 mL) paprika
½ tsp (2.5 mL) salt
½ tsp (2.5 mL) ground cumin
½ tsp (2.5 mL) ground ginger
Pinch or two of cayenne pepper
3 Tbsp (45 mL) canola oil
1½ lb (680 g) bone-in skinless
  chicken thighs

**STEW:**
¾ cup (185 mL) dry green
  lentils
2 Tbsp (30 mL) butter
1½ tsp (7.5 mL) curry powder or
  curry paste
4 to 5 green cardamom pods,
  seeds removed and crushed
  and husks discarded, or
  a pinch or two of ground
  cardamom
2 large onions, diced

3 to 4 garlic cloves, minced
1½ Tbsp (22 mL) grated fresh
  ginger
28 oz (796 mL) can tomatoes
¾ cup (185 mL) yogurt (not
  fat-free)
1½ tsp (7.5 mL) garam masala,
  divided
¼ cup (60 mL) whipping cream
Salt and pepper to taste
Chopped fresh cilantro for
  garnish (optional)

A TAKEOUT FAVOURITE, butter chicken can contain stupefying amounts of fat. Our version is much easier on the arteries, and your wallet too! As with most stews, if you can make this a day or two before eating it, the flavours improve with time. You'll likely need to buy your chicken thighs with skin, and discard it or feed it to the dog.

In a bowl big enough to hold the chicken thighs, combine the marinade ingredients. Add the skinless chicken pieces and coat them well with the spices. Chill while the lentils are cooking, or overnight.

Cook the lentils in 2 cups of water, covered, until soft but not mushy, about 30 to 40 minutes. Drain and set aside.

In a large saucepan, melt 1 Tbsp of the butter over low-moderate heat and brown the chicken, scraping any residual marinade into the pan. Transfer the chicken to a plate. Melt the remaining butter in the same saucepan (don't wash it!) and add the curry powder or curry paste and cardamom seeds. Cook for 1 to 2 minutes, then add the onions. Cook until the onions are transparent, 3 to 4 minutes. Add the garlic and ginger and cook for another 1 to 2 minutes,

CONTINUED . . .

CONTINUED ...

stirring frequently. Add the canned tomatoes with their juices, the yogurt, 1 tsp of the garam masala, the cooked lentils, and the chicken thighs. Bring to a gentle simmer and cook uncovered for 30 minutes.

Using a pair of tongs, transfer the chicken thighs out of the stew to a plate. Carefully pull the meat partially off the bones using a fork and tongs—it will cool much more quickly this way. Once you can handle the chicken, remove and discard the bones, coarsely chop or shred the meat, and return it to the stew. Stir well and add the cream. Taste for seasoning, then spoon over rice. Sprinkle a pinch of garam masala over each serving, and top with chopped cilantro.

# PALAK DAL

### SERVES 6 TO 8.

1 cup (250 mL) dry lentils (any kind—we usually use green)
5 cups (1.25 L) water
1 Tbsp (15 mL) fresh ginger
½ tsp (2.5 mL) turmeric
10 oz (300 g) chopped spinach (fresh or frozen)

2 large tomatoes, chopped, or 1 cup (250 mL) canned diced tomatoes
2 Tbsp (30 mL) butter
1 tsp (5 mL) cumin seeds
½ tsp (2.5 mL) paprika
Pinch or two of cayenne pepper
1 onion, chopped

2 garlic cloves, minced
½ tsp (2.5 mL) salt
½ tsp (2.5 mL) garam masala
2 tsp (10 mL) fresh lemon juice, or more to taste
¼ cup (60 mL) chopped fresh cilantro, for serving

WE'VE ADAPTED THE heat in this dish to make it more child friendly—if that isn't something you need to consider, feel free to boost up the cayenne pepper a little, and maybe add half a finely chopped green chili with the spinach. Leftovers are lovely (and freeze well), and will taste even better on the second day.

In a large pot, bring the lentils, water, ginger, and turmeric to a boil. Lower the heat to a gentle simmer and cook until the lentils are nearly tender, 30 to 35 minutes. Add the spinach and tomatoes and return to a simmer. Cover and cook over low heat (adding a little more water if needed—it should still be a bit soupy) until the lentils are tender, another 10 to 15 minutes. Add the salt.

Once you've added the spinach to the lentils, set a skillet over medium heat. Melt the butter, add the cumin seeds, paprika, and cayenne, and stir until the seeds start to pop and crackle, 1 to 2 minutes. Add the onion and sauté until it softens, 5 to 8 minutes. Add the garlic and cook for 1 more minute. Remove the pan from the heat and let it cool briefly. Scrape up any bits in the skillet, then add the skillet contents to the lentils and spinach. There should still be some liquid in the lentil pot, but if you have more than you want, let it boil down. Stir in the garam masala and lemon juice and let it rest with the heat turned off and the lid on for 10 minutes. Taste for seasoning, then serve over rice or with flatbread, with cilantro sprinkled overtop.

# CHICKEN & BEAN BRAISE

## SERVES 6 TO 8.

**BRAISE:**

2 slices side bacon, diced

1¼ lb (625 g) bone-in skinless chicken thighs

1 large onion, sliced (cut in half at equator, then into slices)

1 large red bell pepper, core removed, sliced in half and then into thin strips

3 garlic cloves, minced

28 oz (796 mL) can diced tomatoes

½ tsp (2.5 mL) dried oregano

½ tsp (2.5 mL) dried basil, or 1 Tbsp (15 mL) minced fresh basil

4 cups (1 L) cooked white beans, or two 19 oz (540 mL) cans, rinsed and drained

Salt and pepper to taste

¼ cup (60 mL) shredded fresh basil for garnish (optional)

**FRIED CAPERS:**

¼ cup (60 mL) olive oil

¼ cup (60 mL) brine-cured small capers (nonpareilles)

BONE-IN THIGHS ARE essential in this stew: don't be tempted to substitute boneless, skinless chicken breast or you'll end up with a sorry and pale imitation. And if you've never been a fan of the caper, give this method a shot! Fried, the capers become delicately crisp and their brininess mellows—some dedicated caper-haters are now seeing things our way. Serve with a chunk of bread or over rice or noodles.

In a large pot with a lid or in a Dutch oven, fry the bacon over low-moderate heat until crispy. Remove to a dinner plate (you'll be adding more ingredients shortly), and drain off all but 1 to 2 Tbsp of fat. Add the chicken thighs to the pan, brown thoroughly on both sides, then remove them to the plate with the bacon. Add the onion and red pepper to the pot and sauté until softened and caramelizing nicely, about 6 to 8 minutes. Add the garlic and cook for 1 more minute. Add the tomatoes with their juices, oregano, basil, beans, a good grinding of pepper, and a little salt. Return the bacon and chicken pieces to the pot and bring the stew to a simmer. As soon as it's bubbling, lower the heat and cover.

(This is a good time to fry up some capers—see below.)

Cook the stew at a bare simmer, stirring 2 or 3 times, for 30 minutes. Transfer the chicken thighs out of the stew to a plate with a pair of tongs, and carefully pull the meat partially off the bones using a fork and tongs—it will cool much

One-Dish Meals

more quickly this way. Once you can handle the chicken, remove and discard the bones, coarsely chop or shred the meat, and return it to the stew. Stir it well and let things heat up again, then scoop into bowls, either over rice or noodles or on its own. Top with the shredded basil and/or fried capers.

TO FRY THE CAPERS: Start by rinsing the capers well, then blotting them dry with a paper towel. If you have time, let them dry for about 30 minutes—if you're short on time, gently press the moisture out using more paper towel. Heat the oil in a small saucepan and fry the capers, swirling them around in the oil occasionally, until they darken and become crisp. This can take as little as 3 minutes and up to 10 minutes. Transfer to paper towels to drain.

*Pasta*

# BAKED MAC & CHEESE
## *with Little White Beans*
### SERVES 6 TO 8.

½ lb (250 g) dry macaroni, whole wheat rotini, small shells, or other pasta

3 Tbsp (45 mL) butter

3 Tbsp (45 mL) all-purpose flour

2½ cups (625 mL) milk

3 cups (750 mL) shredded old white cheddar, Gouda, Monterey Jack, Parmesan, or other meltable cheese

1 cup (250 mL) rinsed and drained canned white beans (half a 19 oz/540 mL can)

**CRUMB TOPPING (OPTIONAL):**

2 slices whole wheat sandwich bread, torn into pieces

2 Tbsp (30 mL) canola oil, olive oil, or melted butter

¼ cup (60 mL) grated Parmesan cheese

EVERYONE NEEDS A good mac and cheese recipe in their repertoire. Soft little white beans from a can are inconspicuous alongside the pasta; alternatively, you could purée them along with some of the milk and stir them into the cheese sauce. This can be made up to 24 hours ahead and refrigerated in the baking dish; sprinkle with the crumb mixture or cheese right before baking.

In a large pot of boiling salted water, cook the pasta until it's tender but not mushy. Set aside.

Preheat the oven to 350°F. In the empty pot, melt the butter over medium heat. Whisk in the flour and cook for a minute or so, until the mixture starts to turn golden. Stir in the milk and bring the sauce to a full boil, whisking constantly. Reduce the heat and simmer for a few minutes, until the mixture is nice and thick.

Remove the sauce from the heat and stir in the cheese until it melts. Add salt to taste, then stir in the drained pasta and beans. If you want a breadcrumb topping, pulse the bread, butter, and Parmesan in a food processor until the bread turns to crumbs and the mixture is well blended. Pour the macaroni and cheese into a baking dish and top with the breadcrumbs or additional cheese.

Bake for 15 to 20 minutes, until the dish is bubbly around the edges and the topping is golden.

# SPAGHETTI
## *with Sausage Meatballs, Tomatoes & Little White Beans*
### SERVES 6.

½ to 1 lb (250 to 500 g)
  spaghetti
Canola or olive oil, for cooking
3 fresh Italian sausages
1 small onion, finely chopped

1 cup (250 mL) rinsed and
  drained canned white beans
  (half a 19 oz/540 mL can)
28 oz (796 mL) can plum
  tomatoes

Salt to taste
¼ cup (60 mL) pesto (optional)
Freshly grated Parmesan
  cheese, for serving

THE EASIEST POSSIBLE way to make meatballs is to squeeze Italian sausage out of its casing at 1-inch intervals—it feels a little like making sausage balloon animals. They hold their shape perfectly, and after browning can finish simmering in tomato sauce, seasoning it as well. Brilliant, no? Now if we could only turn a sausage into a giraffe . . .

Cook the spaghetti according to package directions. Meanwhile, set a large, heavy skillet over medium-high heat and add a drizzle of oil. When it's hot (but not smoking), squeeze the sausage out of its casing into the pan at 1-inch intervals, making meatballs. Stir them around to brown them, but don't worry about cooking them through. Add the onion and cook for a few minutes, until softened and starting to brown. Add the beans and cook for another minute, then add the tomatoes and salt and bring to a simmer.

Cook, breaking up the tomatoes with a spoon and smushing some of the beans as they soften (their starch will help thicken the sauce, too), until the vegetables are soft and the sauce thickens, about 30 minutes. Stir in the pesto, if you're using it. Serve over spaghetti, with Parmesan cheese grated on top.

# BAKED PENNE
## *with Sausage, Spinach & Beans*
### SERVES 6.

Canola or olive oil, for cooking

1 onion, chopped

3 to 5 garlic cloves, crushed

3 fresh chicken or Italian sausages

28 oz (796 mL) can diced tomatoes

2 cups (500 mL) cooked white beans, or a 19 oz (540 mL) can, rinsed and drained

5.5 oz (156 mL) can tomato paste

¼ cup (60 mL) pesto (optional)

Salt and pepper to taste

3 cups (750 mL) dry penne, rigatoni, or rotini pasta (preferably a whole wheat or brown rice variety)

10 oz (300 g) bag baby spinach leaves, coarsely torn

1½ cups (375 mL) shredded mozzarella

½ to 1 cup (125 to 250 mL) grated Parmesan cheese

CHUNKY BAKED PASTA with cheese is pretty close to the top of the list of comfort foods in our book; this one is easy to freeze in smaller baking dishes you can pop in the oven when you don't have time to cook. There's really no reason you couldn't use any kind of bean in here. White beans are right at home with pasta, wilted spinach, tomatoes, and cheese. Feel free to do your own thing—use chard or kale, or leave out the greens altogether and add whatever you particularly like in your pasta.

In a large saucepan, heat a drizzle of oil over medium-high heat and cook the onion and garlic for a few minutes, until soft. Squeeze the sausages out of their casings into the pan and cook, breaking up the meat until it's no longer pink. Add the tomatoes, beans, and tomato paste and simmer for 5 to 10 minutes, until the sauce thickens. Stir in the pesto and some salt and pepper.

Cook the pasta until al dente, drain it well, and toss it with the spinach, mozzarella, and about half the Parmesan cheese in a large bowl. Stir in the hot tomato sauce, which will slightly wilt the spinach. Pour into one or more baking dishes (it should be enough to fill one 9- × 13-inch pan) and sprinkle with the remaining Parmesan. (At this point the dish can be cooled completely, covered, and kept in the refrigerator overnight, or frozen for up to 4 months. Bake from frozen.)

Bake at 350°F for about 30 minutes (40 minutes if frozen), until bubbly and golden.

# PASTA E FAGIOLI (FAZOOL)

## SERVES 4 TO 6.

Canola or olive oil, for cooking
1 small onion, chopped
2 garlic cloves, crushed
 or chopped
1 carrot, peeled and chopped
1 stalk celery, chopped
1 cup (250 mL) cooked white
 kidney, navy, cannellini,

or pinto beans, or half
 a 19 oz (540 mL) can, rinsed
 and drained
2 cups (500 mL) chicken, beef,
 or vegetable stock
14 oz (398 mL) can diced,
 whole, stewed, or crushed
 tomatoes

½ tsp (2.5 mL) dried oregano
 or Italian seasoning
Salt and pepper to taste
½ cup (125 mL) dry small pasta,
 such as shells
Grated Parmesan cheese,
 for serving

DEAN MARTIN MADE this stuff famous in his '50s hit "That's Amore," pronouncing it "pasta fazool." (It's more accurately pronounced pasta *fah-JO-lie*, but fazool is just as recognizable, if not technically correct.) Pasta e Fagioli translates to pasta and beans. You couldn't get further up our alley. (Hmm. That sounded dirty.)

In a medium pot, heat a drizzle of oil over medium-high heat. Sauté the onion, garlic, carrot, and celery for about 5 minutes, until soft.

Mash the beans roughly with a fork (if using canned beans, you can do this right in the open can); add to the pot along with the stock, tomatoes, oregano, and salt and pepper.

Bring to a simmer and add the pasta; cook for 10 minutes, or until the pasta is tender. If the mixture is too thick, add a little extra stock or water—it can be as thick or soupy as you like. Season with more salt and pepper, if needed, and serve hot, preferably with grated Parmesan.

# SPAGHETTI CARBONARA
## *with Caramelized Onions & Peas*
### SERVES 4.

1 lb (500 g) dry spaghetti
½ cup (125 mL) frozen green
    peas or shelled edamame, or
    cooked beans of your choice
4 to 8 slices bacon, chopped

Canola oil, for cooking
    (optional)
1 small onion, halved and thinly
    sliced
3 eggs

½ to 1 cup (125 to 250 mL)
    freshly grated Parmesan
    cheese
Freshly ground black pepper

THERE'S A WHOLE LOT you can do with a bowl of pasta carbonara. Peas are a great fit (they're legumes too!), and you can shake some out of the bag straight from the freezer into the pasta water for the last few minutes of cooking time, then drain it all together. Easy peasy. (Pun totally intended.) If you're not a pea person, cooked small white beans are fine, too. If you don't want onions, try sautéed mushrooms.

In a large pot, boil the spaghetti in lots of water until al dente, adding the peas to the cooking water about five minutes before the spaghetti is done. Before draining, set aside about ½ cup of the cooking liquid.

Meanwhile, cook the bacon until crisp; transfer with a slotted spoon to a plate. If you like, toss out the drippings and add some canola oil to the pan to sauté your onion—either way, cook the onion for 5 to 7 minutes, until golden.

In a small bowl, stir the eggs together with a fork. As soon as the pasta is done, drain it and return it to the warm pot. Pour the eggs overtop and add the cheese, bacon, and onion. Set over low heat and toss with tongs, adding a little reserved pasta water if you like, until the eggs are cooked (they will be after a minute as long as the pasta is still steaming) and the pasta is as saucy as you like it. Season with pepper, but hold off on the salt—the cheese is probably salty enough.

Serve immediately.

# SPAGHETTI WITH GARLIC,

## *Chickpeas & Braised Kale or Chard*

### SERVES 4 TO 6.

½ to 1 lb (250 to 500 g)
   spaghetti or other pasta
   shape
Canola or olive oil, for cooking
1 Tbsp (15 mL) butter (optional)
1 large onion, chopped

2 cups (500 mL) cooked
   chickpeas, or a 19 oz
   (540 mL) can, rinsed and
   well drained
1 garlic bulb, cloves peeled
   and chopped

1 large bunch of kale
Juice of half a lemon
Grated Parmesan cheese
Salt and pepper to taste

ROASTED CHICKPEAS and chard go marvellously over pasta. In fact, this would probably be as delicious with quinoa, barley, or brown rice as well—or swap the Parmesan for other intensely flavoured cheeses, like aged Gouda or Asiago. Who says you have to start your spaghetti sauce with a pound of ground?

Put a big pot of water on to boil, and cook the spaghetti. Meanwhile, heat a generous drizzle of oil in a heavy skillet, add the butter, if you're using it, and sauté the onion and chickpeas for about 10 minutes, until soft and starting to turn golden. Add the garlic and cook for a few more minutes. Scoop out the chickpeas and set them aside in a bowl (don't worry about getting all the onions—you just want to keep your chickpeas somewhat crisp).

Meanwhile, rinse the kale, discard the tough ribs, and coarsely chop or tear the leaves; add the kale to the skillet. Scoop out about ¼ cup of the pasta water, straight from the pot, and add it to the skillet. Cover the skillet, reduce the heat to medium-low, and cook for about 10 minutes, until tender.

Drain the spaghetti, reserving a bit of the cooking liquid. Add the spaghetti to the kale mixture. Add the lemon juice and a few spoonfuls of the reserved cooking liquid; toss to combine. Add the chickpeas and a handful of Parmesan cheese and toss until well combined—add more cooking liquid if you like it saucier. Season with salt and pepper and serve immediately.

*Spilling the Beans*

# SOBA NOODLES WITH MUSHROOM
## *& Lentil Cream Sauce*
### SERVES 4 AS A MAIN, OR 6 AS A STARTER.

**SAUCE:**

½ cup (125 mL) dry lentils (little chestnut brown lentils are nice here; green are fine too)

1 bay leaf

1 garlic clove, peeled and left whole

1 lb (500 g) mushrooms sliced (any kind, but a few wild mushrooms are nice)

1 large or 2 to 3 small shallots, finely chopped

1 Tbsp (15 mL) olive oil

1 Tbsp (15 mL) butter

2 to 3 garlic cloves, minced

1 cup (250 mL) whipping cream

½ cup (125 mL) grated Parmesan, plus more for serving

Salt and pepper to taste

½ lb (250 g) soba noodles (other pasta will substitute well, but soba is a nice change and complements the mushrooms and lentils)

Finely chopped fresh parsley (optional)

WE LOVE IT WHEN indulgent meals are also nutrient-dense. This dish can very nicely satisfy a craving for Fettucini Alfredo, and while both are laden with cream, the comparison ends there. The serving sizes are a little smaller than usual, but it's a very filling combination. If you wish to make the sauce ahead of time, be sure to reheat it gently in a pan large enough to accommodate the pasta. Add a couple tablespoons of liquid if you need to, then add the cooked pasta to the pan.

In a medium saucepan, cook the lentils in 2 cups of water with the bay leaf and whole clove of garlic until soft but not mushy, about 30 to 40 minutes, adding more water if needed. Discard the bay leaf and garlic when done.

Cook the pasta in a large pot of boiling water, then drain and set aside (be aware that soba usually cooks in about 5 to 6 minutes).

Make the sauce while the pasta is cooking: in a large skillet over medium heat, sauté the mushrooms and shallots in olive oil and butter with a little salt until the liquid from the mushrooms has evaporated and everything is browned, 7 to 10 minutes. Add the minced garlic and cook for 1 more minute, then pour in the cream and allow to boil until slightly thickened, scraping any bits stuck to the pan into the sauce. Add the cooked lentils, Parmesan, and salt and pepper, then add the cooked soba noodles and cook for another 2 to 3 minutes. Transfer to serving dishes and top with additional Parmesan and parsley.

Pasta

# BROWN RICE PASTA
## with Mushrooms, Prosciutto & Sprouted Beans
SERVES 2 TO 3.

6 oz (175 g) brown rice pasta,
  or 4 oz (125 g) wheat pasta
1 Tbsp (15 mL) olive oil
4 slices (about 2 oz/60 g)
  prosciutto, sliced crosswise
  into strips
4 oz (125 g) mushrooms,
  cleaned and sliced

2 garlic cloves, minced
3 to 4 big handfuls of fresh
  spinach, torn into pieces if
  the leaves are large
⅔ cup (160 mL) chicken or
  vegetable stock
4 Roma tomatoes, chopped
  (or one 14 oz/398 mL can
  diced tomatoes in juice)

1 cup (250 mL) mixed sprouted
  beans (half an 8oz/225 g
  container)
¼ cup (60 mL) whipping cream
1 Tbsp (15 mL) chopped fresh
  parsley, or 2 Tbsp (30 mL)
  slivered fresh basil (optional)
Black pepper to taste

THIS ISN'T AT ALL difficult to prepare, but it'll make you look like a rock star. For minimal fuss, assemble and measure your ingredients before you start; once you're cooking, things happen quickly.

Boil a large pot of water and cook the pasta according to package directions. Reserve about ½ cup of the cooking water and then drain in a colander.

While the pasta is cooking, set a large skillet over medium heat. Add the olive oil and sauté the prosciutto until slightly crisped and remove to a plate. Add the mushrooms and sauté until browned; add the garlic and spinach and cook until the spinach is wilted. Remove to the same plate as the prosciutto. Add the stock to the pan and turn the heat up. Boil until the stock is reduced to about ¼ cup, then add the tomatoes and sprouted beans. Cover and cook until the beans are tender, 3 to 4 minutes.

Remove the lid and add the cream. Add the cooked pasta, prosciutto, mushrooms, and spinach. Stir well, ensuring everything is coated with sauce, and adding a little of the pasta's cooking water if needed to keep things saucy. Once heated through, divide between serving bowls. Top with parsley or basil and a good grinding of black pepper.

# SPAGHETTI CACIO E PEPE E FAGIOLI

## SERVES 4 TO 6.

½ to 1 lb (250 to 500 g) spaghetti

¼ cup (60 mL) extra virgin olive oil

2 to 3 tsp (10 to 15 mL) freshly ground black pepper, or to taste

1 cup (250 mL) cooked white beans or black-eyed peas,

or half a 19 oz (540 mL) can, rinsed and drained

1 cup (250 mL) freshly grated Parmesan, Pecorino, or Romano cheese, plus extra for serving

OK, WE MAY HAVE completely butchered the name of this one, not actually being fluent in Italian. But it does sound mighty sophisticated, doesn't it? Pasta Cacio e Pepe is a classic but utterly simple Italian dish (translation: cheese and pepper pasta) to which we added—what else?—beans (fagioli). The pepper must be freshly ground—it's toasted first in olive oil to maximize flavour and infuse the oil with pepperiness. Any small white bean or black-eyed peas work well in this. Feel free to play around with other intensely flavoured cheeses as well.

In a large pot of salted water, cook the pasta according to package directions. Before draining, reserve a cup of the cooking water.

Meanwhile, heat the oil in a large, heavy skillet set over medium-high heat and grind in the pepper. Cook for a few minutes, until the pepper is fragrant. Add the beans and cook for a few minutes, to heat through; add the pasta and toss, adding the cheese and pasta water until you have a nice, creamy sauce.

Serve immediately, topped with extra cheese and pepper, if you like.

# ROASTED SQUASH,
## *Garlic, Mushroom & White Bean Lasagna*
### SERVES 8.

**FILLING:**

1 medium butternut squash, peeled and cut into ½-inch chunks

1 garlic bulb, cloves separated and peeled

Canola or olive oil, for cooking

1 large onion, finely chopped

1 Tbsp (15 mL) butter

2 cups (500 mL) sliced mushrooms

1 sprig fresh rosemary, leaves pulled off the stem and chopped (optional)

Salt and pepper to taste

¼ cup (60 mL) all-purpose flour

4 cups (1 L) milk

1 to 2 cups (250 to 500 mL) cooked white beans, or half to a full 19 oz (540 mL) can, rinsed and drained

½ cup (125 mL) grated Parmesan cheese

9 sheets no-boil lasagna noodles

2 cups (500 mL) grated mozzarella

THIS IS A HEARTY, rustic lasagna made with layers of sweet roasted squash, sautéed mushrooms, and little white beans that all but disappear into the creamy sauce. (Don't you love the word "rustic" when applied to food? It excuses—even legitimizes— all imperfections.)

Preheat the oven to 450°F.

Spread the squash and garlic out in a single layer on a rimmed baking sheet and drizzle with oil; toss with your hands to coat well. Sprinkle with salt and pepper and roast for about 20 minutes, until tender and turning golden on the edges.

Meanwhile in a large skillet, heat a drizzle of oil over medium-high heat and sauté the onion for 3 to 4 minutes, until soft. Add the butter, mushrooms, and rosemary, season lightly with salt and pepper, and cook for about 10 more minutes, until the mushrooms have released their liquid, the moisture cooks off, and everything is starting to turn golden.

Sprinkle the flour overtop and cook for a minute, then add the milk, stirring as you pour it in, and bring the mixture

Pasta

to a boil. Reduce the heat and simmer for about
10 minutes, until thickened. Stir in the beans and
Parmesan cheese.

Reduce the oven temperature to 425°F.

Spray a 9- × 13-inch pan with non-stick cooking spray,
or rub it with oil. Put a spoonful of sauce into the bottom
and spread it around (it doesn't need to completely cover
the pan), then add a row of 3 noodles. Top with half the
roasted squash and a third of the sauce; add another row
of 3 noodles, the rest of the squash, and another third
of the sauce, then top with the remaining noodles and
sauce. Cover tightly with tin foil and bake for half an hour.
Remove the tin foil, sprinkle with mozzarella, and bake
for another half an hour, until the noodles are tender and
the cheese is bubbly and golden. Let rest for 20 minutes
before serving.

*Beany Sides*

# ROASTED CHICKPEAS
## *with Garlic & Chard*
SERVES 4 TO 6. (OR 2, IF IT'S US.)

**CHICKPEAS:**
2 cups (500 mL) cooked
  chickpeas, or a 19 oz
  (540 mL) can, rinsed
  and drained well
1 garlic bulb, separated into
  cloves and peeled

2 shallots, 1 small onion,
  or 3 green onions, chopped
⅓ cup (80 mL) olive or
  canola oil

**CHARD:**
Olive or canola oil, for cooking
  (if needed)

1 large bunch chard, centre
  stems removed and leaves
  coarsely torn or chopped
4 garlic cloves, crushed
  (optional)
½ cup (125 mL) chicken, vegetable, or beef broth
Salt and pepper to taste

CHICKPEAS ARE EASY enough to roast in a heavy skillet or in the oven with a skiff of oil. This process is a little more involved, but the result is positively addictive. It may sound garlicky—it is. Adapted from the January 2008 issue of *Bon Appétit*.

Preheat the oven to 400°F.

In a baking dish or cast iron skillet, combine the chickpeas, whole garlic cloves, shallots or onions, and oil. Roast for about 45 minutes, shaking the pan once or twice, until everything is golden.

If you used a cast iron skillet, pour the chickpea mixture into a bowl and set the skillet on the stovetop. Otherwise, pull out a skillet. Drizzle with oil and, when it's hot but not smoking, sauté the chard and crushed garlic for about 5 minutes, until the chard is wilted. Pour the stock overtop, cover, and cook for another 10 minutes, until the chard is tender. Remove the lid and drain any excess liquid away, and/or keep cooking until it evaporates.

Add the chickpea mixture to the pan, season the whole thing with salt and pepper, toss around until heated through, and serve immediately.

# GUINNESS BAKED BEANS

## SERVES 12.

5 slices bacon, chopped (optional)

2 onions, finely chopped

1½ cups (375 mL) ketchup, barbecue sauce, or tomato sauce mixed with ¼ cup (60 mL) packed brown sugar

1 bottle Guinness, or 1¼ cups (310 mL) beef stock, chicken stock, or apple juice

¼ cup (60 mL) apple cider vinegar

¼ cup (60 mL) molasses

¼ cup (60 mL) Dijon, yellow, or grainy mustard

4 cups (1 L) cooked red kidney beans, or two 19 oz (540 mL) cans, rinsed and drained

4 cups (1 L) cooked white beans, or two 19 oz (540 mL) cans, rinsed and drained

Salt and pepper to taste

A few drops of Tabasco sauce (optional)

HA—WE COULDN'T PUT a bean book together without including a big ol' pot of baked beans, now could we? Here it is. Thick and sweet and tangy and everything we think baked beans should be, plus the beer. (Feel free to swap apple juice or stock if there's no beer in the refrigerator, or if other members of the household protest its use this way.) A slow cooker is ideal for this—there really is no better potpourri.

Preheat the oven to 350°F.

In a medium ovenproof saucepan, sauté the bacon over medium heat until crisp. Remove it from the pan, crumble, and set aside. If you're not using bacon, heat a drizzle of canola or olive oil in the pan and sauté the onions in the oil or bacon drippings for about 5 minutes, until tender and beginning to turn golden.

Add the ketchup, Guinness, vinegar, molasses, mustard, beans, and salt and pepper and bring the mixture to a simmer. Put the pan in the oven and bake for 1 hour, stirring once or twice, until it's thickened and bubbly. (Alternatively, transfer the mixture to a baking dish, or put everything in the slow cooker and cook on low for 6 hours.)

Stir the bacon back into the beans about 15 minutes before serving. Add a few shots of Tabasco sauce if you like, and serve the beans hot.

# MAPLE BAKED BEANS

## SERVES 6 TO 8.

½ small onion, finely grated or puréed with a little water
½ cup (125 mL) maple syrup
2 Tbsp (30 mL) sugar
2 Tbsp (30 mL) molasses
2 Tbsp (30 mL) Dijon mustard
2 Tbsp (30 mL) tomato paste

1 garlic clove, minced
Pinch or two of cayenne pepper
¼ to ½ tsp (1 to 2.5 mL) salt if you're using canned beans, a little more if you're using dry
Black pepper to taste

6 cups (1.5 L) cooked white or kidney beans, or three 19 oz (540 mL) cans, rinsed and drained
2 thick slices of side bacon, left whole

YOU CAN USE ALMOST any kind of bean in this recipe. Smaller varieties will take on the flavour of the sauce more readily, but you can use larger ones if you want—just increase the cooking time (and keep an eye on the liquid in the pot). If you want to use dry beans here, you'll need about a pound to make up 6 cups of cooked beans (you may have extra; just use them all). Read up on how to soak and cook your beans on page 6. This recipe doubles easily (and freezes well) if you're providing for a crowd.

Preheat the oven to 300°F.

In a large Dutch oven, or an oven-safe pot with a lid, stir together the onion, maple syrup, sugar, molasses, mustard, tomato paste, garlic, cayenne, salt, and black pepper. Add the beans and stir well to coat. Pour boiling water overtop until the beans are just covered. If the pot is safe for the stovetop, bring to a gentle simmer over medium heat (this step will save a little oven time). Slide the bacon into the middle of the beans, cover the pot, and transfer to the oven.

Bake for 4 to 5 hours, checking hourly to ensure the beans are still covered, and topping up with more water if necessary. When the sauce has thickened and the beans have taken on the colour and flavour of the sauce, remove the bacon altogether, or chop it fine and stir it back in.

# WHITE BEAN MASHED POTATOES

## SERVES 6.

2 lb (1 kg) Yukon Gold or russet potatoes, peeled and diced

2 cups (500 mL) rinsed and drained canned white beans (19 oz/540 mL can)

½ cup (125 mL) milk or half-and-half

¼ cup (60 mL) butter, or to taste

Salt and pepper to taste

WE LIKE MASHING Yukon Golds, but russets work fine too. Yukon Gold potatoes are buttery to begin with, so you're ahead of the game from the get-go. They aren't as absorbent as russets, so won't soak up as much butter and cream, if you're trying to be stingy in that area. Canned beans are best here, as they tend to purée more smoothly than simmered dry beans. (If you use dry beans, simmer them with a clove of garlic, and overcook them so that they mush easily.) If you really don't want to detect them, give them a buzz in the food processor first.

Cover the potatoes with water in a large pot and bring to a boil; cook for about 15 minutes, until tender. Drain and add the beans, milk, butter, and salt and pepper. Mash with a potato masher until it's as smooth as you like.

# CHARD, WHITE BEAN
## *& Sweet Potato Gratin*
### SERVES 6.

Canola or olive oil, for cooking
1 small onion, finely chopped
2 bunches chard, leaves and
  stems separated and both cut
  into 1-inch pieces
2 Tbsp (30 mL) butter
2 Tbsp (30 mL) all-purpose
  flour

2 cups (500 mL) milk
2 garlic cloves, crushed
Salt and pepper to taste
1 large dark-fleshed sweet
  potato, peeled and sliced
  ⅛ inch thick

2 cups (500 mL) cooked white
  beans, or a 19 oz (540 mL)
  can, rinsed and drained
Freshly grated nutmeg
1 cup (250 mL) coarsely
  shredded Gruyère, old
  cheddar, or Gouda cheese

YOU KNOW SCALLOPED potatoes? This is like scalloped potatoes, with character. It's heavenly. Although it would be perfectly appropriate to serve this alongside a roast chicken or the like, it also fits the bill as dinner on its own. (Anytime we've made it we've eaten enough to calorically count as dinner.) In fact, neither of us recall ever having leftovers. It's pretty fab with a bit of finely chopped rosemary thrown in with the onion, too.

Heat a drizzle of oil in a heavy skillet set over medium-high heat and cook the onion for a few minutes. Add the chard, sprinkle with salt, and cook until the chard wilts and there is no moisture left in the pan. Transfer to a bowl.

Add the butter and flour to the skillet and whisk together to make a paste. Whisk in the milk, then add the garlic and bring to a simmer. Boil for 2 minutes, whisking; season with salt and pepper and remove from the heat.

Preheat the oven to 400°F. Spray a baking dish with non-stick cooking spray. Spread half of the sweet potatoes in the baking dish. Top with half the beans, a sprinkle of nutmeg, salt and pepper, half of the greens mixture, half the cheese, and half the sauce. Layer with the rest of the potatoes, beans, greens, and sauce, and top with the rest of the cheese.

Cover with tin foil and bake for about 45 minutes, then take the tin foil off and bake for another 15 minutes, until golden and bubbly. Let stand 15 minutes before serving.

# LENTILS BRAISED IN RED WINE

## SERVES 4 TO 6.

| | | |
|---|---|---|
| 2 slices bacon, finely diced | 1 cup (250 mL) dry lentils | 1 Tbsp (15 mL) tomato paste |
| 1 large shallot, finely diced | (green are fine; brown or blue | 1 cup (250 mL) beef stock |
| ½ celery stalk, finely diced | are nice too) | 1½ cups (375 mL) water |
| 1 small carrot, finely diced | 1 bay leaf | Salt and pepper to taste |
| 1 garlic clove, minced | ⅔ cup (160 mL) red wine | |

A LIGHTER VERSION OF the Lentil & Mushroom Bourguignon on page 154, this pairs nicely with a rich main such as lamb chops or a roast chicken with vegetables. Add salt cautiously: the bacon and stock bring a lot of salt to this already.

Sauté the diced bacon in a medium saucepan over low to medium heat until browned and crisp. Transfer to a small bowl. Remove and discard all but a spoonful of the fat remaining in the saucepan, and in it sauté the shallot, celery, and carrot until softened slightly, 3 to 5 minutes. Stir in the garlic and cook another 2 minutes, then add the lentils, bay leaf, red wine, tomato paste, beef stock, and water.

Bring just to a boil, then reduce the heat and simmer with the lid on for about 45 to 55 minutes, until the lentils are done. Check occasionally, and add a little more water as needed if it seems dry. Season with salt and pepper.

This can be prepared ahead of time, but you may want a little more broth and a small drizzle of oil when you reheat the lentils, as they tend to absorb more liquid over time.

# EASY RED LENTIL DAL

### SERVES 4 TO 6.

Canola or olive oil, for cooking
1 small onion, finely chopped
1 Tbsp (15 mL) grated fresh
   ginger
2 garlic cloves, crushed

1 tsp (5 mL) curry paste or
   powder
½ cup (125 mL) dry red lentils
2 cups (500 mL) water,
   or 1 cup water plus 1 cup
   chicken or vegetable stock

Salt and pepper to taste
¼ cup (60 mL) whipping cream,
   or 1 Tbsp (15 mL) butter

ADD ANY NUMBER OF spices you like to this—chili powder, cumin, turmeric, garam masala . . . or add a finely chopped fresh chili or pinch of dried red chili flakes to bump up the heat. It's perfect when you need a side of beans, without the barbecue theme.

Drizzle some oil into a large skillet set over medium-high heat and sauté the onion for 3 to 4 minutes, until starting to turn golden. Add the ginger, garlic, and curry paste and cook for another minute.

Add the lentils and water and bring to a boil. Turn the heat down to medium-low and simmer for about half an hour, until the lentils are soft and the liquid has almost been absorbed. If it's too dry, add a little extra stock or water.

Season with salt and pepper and stir in the cream or butter. Serve immediately.

# Baking with Beans

THIS SECTION DOES NEED A LITTLE bit of a preface, just to get you comfortable with the idea of baking with beans. It is a little unconventional. But it works wonderfully.

Baked goods in general are not known for their stellar nutrient content. Using whole-grain flours helps, but we discovered that puréeing beans and adding cooked red lentils to doughs and batters boosts nutritional value far more than even the grainiest of grains. Case in point: I cup of kidney beans contains over 13 grams of fibre. Comparatively, a cup of dry rolled oats contains 8 grams. Of course there's a whole lot more to a bean than just fibre, but we've filled you in on their myriad benefits already. Bonus: the flour present in baked goods, combined with beans, makes a complete protein.

Because beans are so benign in flavour, they blend right in and are virtually unde-tectable, particularly to the pint-sized palate.

And really, if you can make baked goods like cakes, cookies, and scones that much health-ier while retaining their full deliciousness, why not?

Aesthetically, we prefer to use white beans. Canned white kidney (or navy) beans, rinsed and well drained, are the ones we most often bake with around here. Canned beans are plumper, softer, and easier to purée to abso-lute smoothness—after all, if anyone finds a kidney bean in their cookie, the jig is up. If you do start with dry beans, overcook them to the point where they're almost mushy, then purée them with some of their cooking water to help them along. In other cases, dry red lentils are brilliant—they come across as oats in a recipe, blending right in to scones and textured cookies and cakes. Try simmering some and adding them to your own favourite recipes.

Baking with Beans

# CHOCOLATE CUPCAKES

MAKES 2 DOZEN CUPCAKES.

1¾ cups (435 mL) all-purpose
flour
1 cup (250 mL) packed brown
sugar
¾ cup (185 mL) unsweetened
cocoa powder
1 tsp (5 mL) baking powder

1 tsp (5 mL) baking soda
¼ tsp (1 mL) salt
1 cup (250 mL) rinsed and
drained canned white beans
or brown lentils (half a
19 oz/540 mL can)
½ cup (125 mL) canola oil

2 large eggs
1 cup (250 mL) milk
2 tsp (10 mL) vanilla
1 tsp (5 mL) instant coffee
dissolved in 1 cup (250 mL)
water

YES, CHOCOLATE
cupcakes work well as delicious little Trojan horses
for nutrient-dense beans.
No one will suspect a thing.
Coffee makes a deeper,
more intensely flavoured
chocolate cake; if you're
worried about caffeine,
decaf is fine. Or swap it
with a cup of orange juice
or milk. If it's a whole cake
you're after, bake the batter in two 9-inch round
cake pans for 30 minutes.

Preheat the oven to 350°F. Line a 24-cup muffin pan with
paper liners (or do 12 at a time).

In a large bowl, whisk together the flour, brown sugar,
cocoa, baking powder, baking soda, and salt, breaking up
any lumps of brown sugar and cocoa.

In the bowl of a food processor, pulse the beans, oil, and
eggs until well blended; add the milk and vanilla and pulse
until smooth. Add to the dry ingredients along with the
coffee and whisk until combined.

Divide the batter among the tins, filling them about ¾ full,
and bake for 25 minutes, until the tops are springy to the
touch. Tip them a bit in their cups to let the steam escape
and help them cool. Cool completely before frosting.

# OATMEAL RAISIN SCONES

## MAKES 8 TO 12 SCONES.

¼ cup (60 mL) dry red lentils

1½ cups (375 mL) all-purpose flour

½ cup (125 mL) oats, old-fashioned or quick-cooking

¼ cup (60 mL) packed brown sugar

2 tsp (10 mL) baking powder

¼ tsp (1 mL) baking soda

¼ tsp (1 mL) salt

⅓ cup (80 mL) cold butter, cut into chunks

½ cup (125 mL) raisins or currants

½ cup (125 mL) buttermilk

1 large egg

Coarse sugar, for sprinkling (optional)

IT TOOK A FEW TRIES to come up with a scone that contained legumes but didn't have the consistency of a doorstop—we succeeded with cooked red lentils that disguise themselves nicely as oats in these light-crumbed wedge scones. When we shared them with friends, some declared them the best scones ever (OK, maybe they were just trying to be nice, but we'll take it). Regardless, no one guessed that they contained lentils. They're wonderful served warm, spread with jam. Feel free to swap the raisins with other dried fruit, or add a cup of fresh or frozen (don't thaw them) berries.

In a small saucepan, cover the red lentils with water by an inch or two and bring to a simmer; cook for 15 minutes, until soft. Drain well and set aside.

Preheat the oven to 400°F.

In a bowl or the bowl of a food processor, combine the flour, oats, brown sugar, baking powder, baking soda, and salt. Add the butter and pulse or blend with a fork or pastry blender until well combined, with pieces of butter the size of peas remaining. If you used a food processor, transfer to a bowl. Add the raisins and drained lentils and toss a bit.

In a small bowl, stir the buttermilk and egg together with a fork. Add to the flour mixture and stir with a spatula just until combined. Turn the dough out onto a baking sheet that has been sprayed with non-stick cooking spray or lined with parchment, and pat into a circle about 1 inch thick.

Sprinkle with coarse sugar and cut into 8 to 12 wedges with a sharp knife. Pull each wedge apart, leaving about an inch of space between them. Bake for 20 minutes, or until golden.

Baking with Beans

# PUMPKIN CHOCOLATE CHIP
## *Loaf Cake*
### MAKES 2 LOAVES.

¼ cup (60 mL) dry red lentils

2½ cups (625 mL) all-purpose flour

1 cup (250 mL) sugar (white or brown)

1½ tsp (7.5 mL) ground cinnamon

½ tsp (2.5 mL) ground ginger

1 tsp (5 mL) baking powder

1 tsp (5 mL) baking soda

¼ tsp (1 mL) salt

14 oz (398 mL) can puréed pumpkin

½ cup (125 mL) canola oil

½ cup (125 mL) buttermilk, thin plain yogurt, or milk

3 large eggs

1 tsp (5 mL) vanilla

½ to 1 cup (125 to 250 mL) chocolate chips, chopped walnuts or pecans, or a combination

AS IT TURNS OUT, RED lentils get along very well with pumpkin. They fit right into a moist, mildly spiced loaf-sort-of-cake, studded with chocolate chips, which fueled us through many a long hour of editing this book. Thanks, red lentil pumpkin cake. (P.S.: this loaf freezes well, too, so you can have one now, and one stashed away in case of a cake emergency.)

Preheat the oven to 350°F. Spray two 8- × 4-inch loaf pans with non-stick cooking spray.

In a small saucepan, cover the lentils with water by an inch or two and bring to a boil. Simmer for 15 minutes, or until soft. Drain.

In a large bowl, stir together the flour, sugar, spices, baking powder, baking soda, and salt. In the bowl of a food processor, combine the lentils, pumpkin, oil, buttermilk, eggs, and vanilla; pulse until well blended and smooth.

Add the wet ingredients to the dry along with the chocolate chips and stir just until combined. Scrape into the prepared pans and bake for an hour, until the tops are cracked and springy to the touch. Cool on a wire rack.

# BANANA BREAD

## MAKES 1 LOAF.

2 very ripe bananas
1 cup (250 mL) rinsed
    and drained canned
    white beans (half a
    19 oz/540 mL can)
¾ cup (185 mL) sugar
¼ cup (60 mL) canola oil

2 large eggs
2 tsp (10 mL) vanilla
1½ cups (375 mL) all-purpose
    flour, or ¾ cup all-purpose
    and ¾ cup whole wheat
1 tsp (5 mL) baking soda

½ tsp (2.5 mL) ground
    cinnamon
¼ tsp (1 mL) salt
½ cup (125 mL) chopped
    walnuts, chocolate chips,
    raisins, or fresh or frozen
    blueberries (optional)

EVERYONE NEEDS A good banana bread recipe in their repertoire. It turns out white beans can slip right in undetected, which is a boon if you are in charge of the care and feeding of anyone who might choose to live exclusively on banana bread if they had the option. The beans make it a slightly more well-rounded snack, and will deliver some protein, too, if the loaf is sent in a school lunch. (It's also great toasted, with peanut butter.)

Preheat the oven to 350°F.

In the bowl of a food processor, pulse the bananas, beans, sugar, oil, eggs, and vanilla until well blended and more or less smooth. (Don't worry about grinding up all the lumps of banana.) Pour into a large bowl.

Add the flour, baking soda, cinnamon, and salt and stir until almost blended; add any additions (nuts, chocolate chips, raisins, or whatever) and stir just until combined.

Spread into an 8- × 4-inch loaf pan that has been sprayed with non-stick cooking spray and bake for 50 to 60 minutes, until golden and cracked on top and springy to the touch.

# ZUCCHINI BREAD

## MAKES 1 LOAF.

1¾ cups (435 mL) flour (entirely all-purpose, or up to half whole wheat if you like)
¾ cup (185 mL) Candied Lentil Meal (see page 260)
¾ cup (185 mL) sugar
1 Tbsp (15 mL) baking powder

½ tsp (2.5 mL) baking soda
½ tsp (2.5 mL) ground cinnamon
¼ tsp (1 mL) salt
½ cup (125 mL) milk
¼ cup (60 mL) canola oil
2 large eggs

Grated zest of 1 lemon
2 cups (500 mL) grated zucchini (about 1 large zucchini)
½ cup (125 mL) chopped walnuts or pecans

WHEN ZUCCHINI starts taking over the farmers' markets, its price drops to ridiculous lows. And because we're both total cheapos, we tend to come home with armloads of them. If you find yourself similarly afflicted, fear not! This bread is packed with nutrients, and smells like heaven while it's baking. It also freezes well, unlike armloads of fresh zucchini. And neighbours will be far happier to see it on their doorstep.

Preheat the oven to 350°F.

In a large bowl, mix the flour, Lentil Meal, sugar, baking powder, baking soda, cinnamon, and salt. In a smaller bowl, whisk together the milk, oil, eggs, and lemon zest. Add the milk mixture, zucchini, and walnuts to the flour mixture, and mix gently by hand until just combined. Don't worry about getting all the lumps out.

Pour into an 8- × 4-inch loaf pan that has been sprayed with non-stick cooking spray, and bake for about an hour, until golden and springy to the touch, or until a toothpick inserted in the middle comes out clean. Cool in the pan on a wire rack.

# CITRUS BLISS POUND CAKE

### MAKES 2 LOAVES.

¾ cup (185 mL) butter, softened

1½ cups (375 mL) sugar, divided

Zest of 2 lemons and 2 oranges

5 large eggs

1 cup (250 mL) rinsed and drained canned white beans (half a 19 oz/540 mL can)

½ cup (125 mL) lemon and orange juice (from the zested fruit)

⅔ cup (160 mL) milk

2½ cups (625 mL) all-purpose flour

1 tsp (5 mL) baking powder

½ tsp (2.5 mL) baking soda

½ tsp (2.5 mL) salt

**SYRUP:**

½ cup (125 mL) sugar

½ cup (125 mL) lemon and orange juice (from the zested fruit)

THE NAME WAS suggested by Sue's daughter Evelyn. How could we say no—and why would we want to? There's plenty of orange and lemon zing here, but you can increase the zest even more if you like. Just be sure to wash and dry your fruit well, then grate the zest as finely as possible, avoiding the bitter white pith—it's no friend at all to your good baking. Oh, and always zest before juicing! It's a little awkward trying to grate a deflated citrus fruit.

Preheat the oven to 350°F.

In a large bowl, beat the butter, 1 cup of the sugar, and the lemon and orange zest until pale and fluffy, about 3 to 4 minutes. Add the eggs one at a time, beating well after each addition. After zesting the lemons and oranges, squeeze their juices into a measuring cup—you should have about 1 cup. If not, top it up with some additional lemon or orange juice.

In the bowl of a food processor, purée the beans with the remaining ½ cup of sugar until perfectly smooth. Add to the butter mixture and beat well.

Add ½ cup of the lemon and orange juices to the milk and let sit for a moment to thicken. In a small bowl, stir together the flour, baking powder, baking soda, and salt. Add about one-third of the dry ingredients to the butter mixture and stir by hand until barely combined. Add half the milk in the same manner, then another third of the flour, the rest of the milk, and the rest of the flour, stirring just until blended.

Divide the batter between two 8- × 4-inch loaf pans that have been sprayed with non-stick cooking spray, and bake for 50 to 60 minutes, until pale golden and springy to the touch, or until a toothpick inserted in the middle comes out clean. Let cool for 5 minutes in the pans on a wire rack.

While the cakes are baking, combine the sugar and remaining juice in a small saucepan and heat just until the sugar dissolves. Spoon evenly over the tops of the barely cooled cakes, then let the cakes cool completely in the pans. You can freeze one of the loaves for a rainy day if you like— but pop it in the freezer unwrapped first. Once it's frozen, you can wrap it up tight. Unwrap before you thaw and cover loosely; this way the sticky top of the cake won't stay behind on the wrapping.

# BLUEBERRY BIG CRUMB CAKE

## SERVES 12 TO 16.

**CAKE:**

1 cup (250 mL) rinsed and
drained canned white beans
(half a 19 oz/540 mL can)
¾ cup (185 mL) sugar
¼ cup (60 mL) butter, softened
¼ cup (60 mL) buttermilk or
thin plain yogurt
2 Tbsp (30 mL) canola oil
2 large eggs

1 tsp (5 mL) vanilla
1½ cups (375 mL) flour
(all-purpose, whole wheat,
or a combination)
1 tsp (5 mL) baking powder
¼ tsp (1 mL) salt
2 to 3 cups (500 to 750 mL)
fresh or frozen (not thawed)
berries, or a few thickly sliced
plums, peaches, or apricots

**CRUMBLE:**

2 Tbsp (30 mL) butter,
softened
2 Tbsp (30 mL) canola oil
¾ cup (185 mL) flour (all-
purpose or whole wheat)
¼ cup (60 mL) sugar
¼ cup (60 mL) packed
brown sugar
¼ cup (60 mL) Candied Red
Lentils (page 259) (optional)
Pinch of salt

ANY FRUIT IN SEASON
goes well in a crumb cake—
peaches, plums, chopped
rhubarb, or fresh or frozen
berries. It's cake on the
bottom, crumble on top—
the best of both worlds.

Preheat the oven to 350°F.

Place the beans in the bowl of a food processor along
with the sugar, butter, buttermilk, oil, eggs, and vanilla,
and pulse until well blended and smooth.

In a medium bowl, stir together the flour, baking powder,
and salt. Add the wet ingredients and stir just until combined; spread into a 9-inch square pan that has been
buttered or sprayed with non-stick cooking spray. Sprinkle
the berries or lay the sliced fruit overtop.

In a small bowl, blend the crumble ingredients, mixing
with a fork or rubbing between your fingers until evenly
combined and crumbly. Sprinkle over the berries, squeezing the mixture in your hands as you go to create bigger
chunks of crumble. Bake for about 1 hour, until golden
and a wooden skewer inserted comes out clean.

# CARROT CAKE

MAKES 1 CAKE (ABOUT 16 SERVINGS).

3 cups (750 mL) all-purpose flour, or a combination of all-purpose and whole wheat

1 cup (250 mL) sugar

1 cup (250 mL) packed brown sugar

1 Tbsp (15 mL) baking soda

2 tsp (10 mL) ground cinnamon

1 tsp (5 mL) salt

2 cups (500 mL) rinsed and drained canned white beans (19 oz/540 mL can)

1 cup (250 mL) canola or olive oil

4 large eggs

1 Tbsp (15 mL) grated fresh ginger, or 1 tsp (5 mL) ground ginger

1 Tbsp (15 mL) vanilla

2 packed cups (500 mL) coarsely grated carrots, beets, sweet potatoes, or a combination (about 3 carrots)

1 cup (250 mL) chopped walnuts, pecans, raisins, or dried cranberries, or a combination of dried fruit and nuts

A DENSE, MOIST carrot cake is the perfect vehicle for a can of beans—they contribute the added moisture that often comes from applesauce or crushed pineapple. To up your bean intake even further, add a handful of Candied Lentil Meal (page 260) along with or instead of the nuts and raisins. This batter also makes delicious carrot muffins, baked in a couple dozen lined or buttered muffin tins for 25 minutes.

Preheat the oven to 325°F. Spray a Bundt pan or two 9-inch round cake pans with non-stick cooking spray.

In a large bowl, stir together the flour, sugars, baking soda, cinnamon, and salt. In the bowl of a food processor, pulse the beans until chunky; add the oil, eggs, ginger, and vanilla and pulse until well blended and smooth.

Add the pureed bean mixture and the grated carrots to the dry ingredients and stir by hand until almost combined. Add the nuts and dried fruit and stir just until the batter is blended.

Pour the batter into the prepared pan(s). Bake for 1 hour and 15 minutes for a Bundt cake, or 40 to 45 minutes for layer cakes, until the tops are cracked and springy to the touch and the edges are pulling away from the sides of the pan. Cool the cake(s) in the pan(s) for 10 to 15 minutes, then loosen the edges with a knife and invert onto a wire rack to cool completely. (If you decide to frost the cake, make sure it's completely cool first, or the frosting will melt and slide down the sides.)

# NAAN

## MAKES 8 TO 10 NAAN.

½ cup (125 mL) warm water
2¼ tsp (11 mL) active dry yeast
(1 package)
1 tsp (5 mL) sugar

1 cup (250 mL) rinsed and
drained canned white beans
(half a 19 oz/540 mL can)
½ cup (125 mL) plain yogurt
¼ cup (60 mL) canola oil
1 large egg, beaten

2¾ to 3 cups (685 to 750 mL)
all-purpose flour, plus extra
as needed
½ tsp (2.5 mL) salt
Canola or olive oil, for cooking
Butter, for cooking (optional)

MOST ANY SAUCY curry is best served with warm naan, a chewy Indian flatbread that's easier to make than you might think. Stir the dough together, let it rise, then roll out rough circles and cook in a hot, heavy skillet; add a drizzle of oil and dab of butter in between frying each naan, for a golden, buttery crust. So worth the effort. The only problem is, very few may actually make it to the table. (Bonus: leftovers make great pizza crusts.)

In a large bowl, stir together the water, yeast, and sugar and let stand for a few minutes, until foamy. If it doesn't foam up a bit, the yeast is inactive—toss it out and buy some fresh yeast.

In the bowl of a food processor, purée the beans with the yogurt, oil, and egg; add to the yeast mixture. Stir in 2½ cups of the flour and the salt and stir until you have a sticky dough. Add more flour, turning the dough out onto a floured surface and kneading it until the dough is smooth and elastic. Cover with a tea towel and let rise until doubled in size, about an hour or two.

Divide the dough into 8 to 10 pieces. On a lightly floured surface, roll out each piece into an oval. Set a heavy skillet over high heat and add a drizzle of oil and, if you like, a pat of butter. When the pan and oil (and butter) are hot, cook one naan at a time until golden on the bottom and blistered on top; flip and cook until golden on the other side as well. Serve immediately, or keep warm in a 250° F oven until ready to serve.

# BRIOCHE BURGER OR SLIDER BUNS

## MAKES 10 BURGER BUNS OR 20 SLIDER BUNS.

½ cup (125 mL) warm water
¼ cup (60 mL) milk
2 Tbsp (30 mL) sugar
2¼ tsp (11 mL) active dry yeast
  (1 package)

1 cup (250 mL) rinsed and
  drained canned white beans
  (half a 19 oz/540 mL can)
1 large egg
3½ cups (875 mL) all-purpose
  flour

1 tsp (5 mL) salt
3 Tbsp (45 mL) butter
Additional egg, for brushing,
  and/or sesame seeds
  (optional)

ISN'T IT RIDICULOUS that we're all expected to build our own decks, paint our own houses, and do our own taxes, yet mixing up a batch of burger buns from scratch is almost unheard of. If you're making burgers—bean-based or not—you may as well up the nutrient content of the buns! These have the soft texture of a good-quality white bun, so no one will know the difference. Make them small if you're doing sliders, and if you just want buns, sans burgers, that's OK too.

In a small bowl, stir together the water, milk, sugar, and yeast. Let it stand for about 5 minutes, until it's foamy. (If it doesn't foam, get some fresh yeast and try again.) Meanwhile, purée the beans with the egg and another ½ cup water in a food processor until smooth.

In a large bowl, stir together the flour and salt; blend in the butter with a pastry blender, whisk, or your fingers, rubbing until it's crumbly. Add the yeast and bean mixtures and stir; beat with a dough hook in your stand mixer or knead on a lightly floured countertop until smooth, 5 to 10 minutes. It will be stickier than regular dough; resist the urge to add too much flour. Leave it tacky. Place the ball of dough back into the bowl, cover it with a tea towel, and let it sit for an hour or so, until doubled.

Divide the dough into 10 to 20 pieces, shape them into balls, and place them a couple inches apart on a baking sheet that has been sprayed with non-stick cooking spray or lined with parchment. Cover loosely with plastic wrap and let rise for another hour.

Preheat the oven to 400°F. Brush the buns with a little beaten egg if you like, and sprinkle them with sesame seeds (if using). Bake for 10 to 15 minutes (a bit longer if you made larger buns), until golden.

# NO-KNEAD BREAD

MAKES 1 LOAF.

1 cup (250 mL) rinsed and drained canned white beans (half a 19 oz/540 mL can)

3 cups (750 mL) all-purpose or bread flour, or a combination of all-purpose and whole wheat, plus more for dusting

½ tsp (2.5 mL) active dry yeast
1 tsp (5 mL) salt

THIS BREAD RECIPE will change your life. Having the ability to almost effortlessly turn out a crusty, warm loaf whenever you want it is earth-shattering enough, but now you can smuggle in beans while maintaining the flavour and texture of white bread. (Thanks to Jim Lahey at the Sullivan Street Bakery in Manhattan for the concept of no-knead bread.) It works well as pizza crust, too.

Put the beans and ½ cup water into the bowl of a food processor and purée until smooth.

In a large bowl, stir together the flour, yeast, and salt. Add the beans along with 1 cup of water and stir until blended; the dough will be shaggy and sticky. Cover the bowl with plastic wrap or a plate and let it rest on the countertop for 18 to 24 hours at room temperature.

The dough is ready when its surface is dotted with bubbles. Flour a work surface and place the dough on it; sprinkle the dough with a little more flour, fold it over on itself once or twice, then roughly shape it into a ball. Generously coat a cotton towel (preferably a smooth one—terry cloth will stick) with flour. Place the dough on the towel and dust with more flour. Fold the towel over the bread, or cover with another cotton towel, and let it sit for another hour or two.

While the bread is resting, preheat the oven to 450°F. Put a 6- to 8-quart heavy covered pot (cast iron, enamel, Pyrex, or ceramic) into the oven as it heats.

CONTINUED . . .

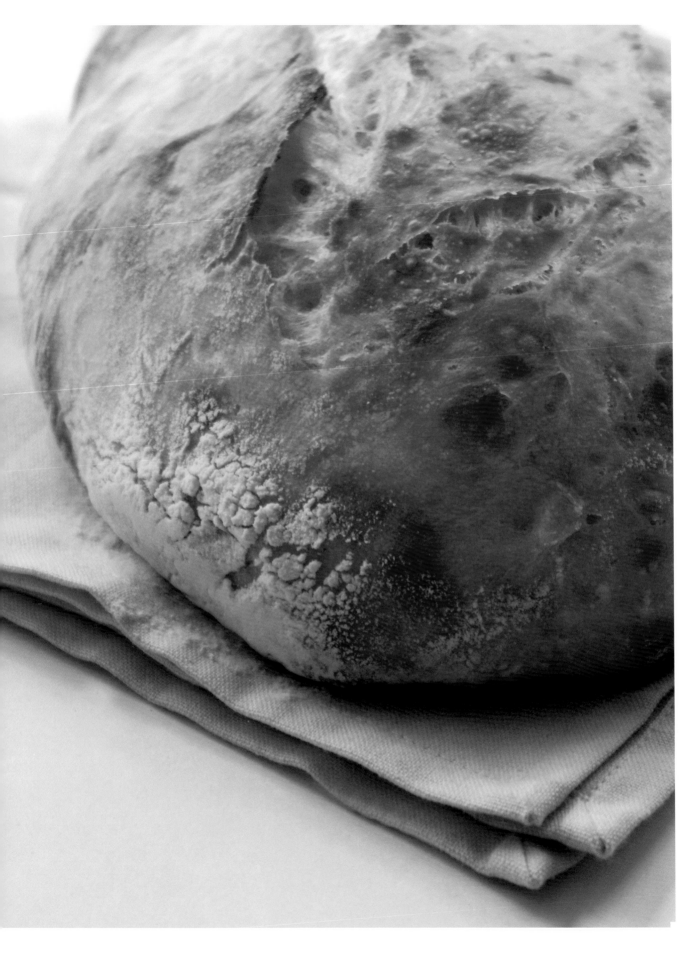

CONTINUED... When the dough is ready, carefully remove the pot from the oven. Slide your hand under the towel and flip the dough over into the pot; it may look like a mess, but that's OK. Cover and bake for 30 minutes, then remove the lid and bake another 10 to 15 minutes, until it's crusty and golden.

**NO-KNEAD PIZZA DOUGH:**
Spread the sticky risen dough out onto a floured or cornmeal-dusted rimmed baking sheet (it can be divided in two if you don't want a pizza that large). Bake at 450°F for about 10 minutes, or until set and starting to turn golden; spread with sauce and scatter with toppings and cheese, then return to the oven for another 10 to 15 minutes, until the crust is golden and the cheese is melted.

# PRETZELS

MAKES 10 TO 12 PRETZELS.

2¼ tsp (11 mL) active dry yeast
   (1 package)
¾ cup (185 mL) lukewarm
   water
1 tsp (5 mL) sugar
2 cups (500 mL) rinsed and
   drained canned white beans
   (19 oz/540 mL can)

¾ cup (185 mL) lukewarm milk
2 Tbsp (30 mL) canola oil
4½ to 5 cups (1 to 1.25 L) all-
   purpose flour
1 tsp (5 mL) salt
Coarse sea salt or sesame seeds,
   for sprinkling

**BOILING SOLUTION:**
8 cups (2 L) water
2 Tbsp (30 mL) baking soda
1 Tbsp (15 mL) salt

OUR KIDS LOVE making these, although they rarely wind up in remotely pretzel-esque shapes. They're easier than you might think to make from scratch—adding puréed kidney beans contributes extra nutrients, protein, and fibre, making them a more well-rounded snack (or lunch box addition) than straight-up bread. Boiling before baking gives pretzels their dense, chewy texture. To make pizza pretzels, spread boiled pretzels with thick tomato sauce or paste, then sprinkle with grated cheese before baking. To make bagels, shape them like a bagel and boil, then bake the same way.

In a large bowl, stir the yeast and sugar into the water; let it sit for about 10 minutes. If it's not foamy, toss it out and buy fresh yeast.

In a food processor, blend the beans, milk, and canola oil until smooth; add to the yeast. Stir in 3 cups of the flour and the salt. Add the rest of the flour ½ cup at a time. When it becomes difficult to stir, turn it out onto a floured countertop. Knead, adding extra flour if it's too sticky, for about 8 minutes, until the dough is smooth and elastic. Cover with a tea towel and let rest for an hour.

Cut the dough into 10 pieces and roll each into a rope. Shape each piece into a pretzel, set aside on a baking sheet, and let rest for 15 minutes while you bring 2 litres of water to a rolling boil with the baking soda and salt.

Preheat the oven to 425°F. Boil 2 to 3 pretzels at a time so you don't crowd the pot (they will swell) and simmer for a minute per side, flipping them over with a slotted spoon. Remove from the water with the spoon and place on a baking sheet that has been sprayed with non-stick cooking spray. Sprinkle with coarse salt as soon as they come out of the water, so that it sticks. Bake for 20 minutes, until golden.

*Spilling the Beans*

# PIZZA DOUGH (& FOCACCIA)

MAKES ENOUGH DOUGH FOR TWO TO THREE 10-INCH PIZZAS.

1 cup (250 mL) rinsed and drained canned white beans (half a 19 oz/540 mL can)

1 cup (250 mL) warm water, divided

2¼ tsp (11 mL) active dry yeast (1 package)

1 tsp (5 mL) sugar

2½ cups (625 mL) flour, either entirely all-purpose or half whole wheat (approximate—you may need a little more or less)

1 tsp (5 mL) salt

2 Tbsp (30 mL) olive or canola oil

Additional oil, coarse salt, and chopped fresh rosemary (optional; for focaccia)

THE FIRST TIME you make pizza dough you'll feel like a super-hero, but it's dead easy.

Start by puréeing the beans with about ¼ cup of the water until completely smooth.

In a large bowl, stir together the remaining warm water, yeast, and sugar. The mixture should get foamy after a few minutes—if it doesn't, it means the water was too hot and killed the yeast, or you need fresh yeast. Try again, or buy fresh yeast.

Add the puréed beans to the yeast mixture along with 1 cup of flour. Mix thoroughly, then add another cup of flour, the salt, and the oil. Again, mix thoroughly. Continue to add flour by ½ cups, and as soon as the batter is thick enough to make a kneadable dough, turn it out onto a floured counter. Knead until the dough is smooth and elastic, adding spoonfuls of flour if needed, until the dough has lost most of its stickiness.

Wash out the bowl, dry it, and add a small splash of oil. Return the dough to the bowl, turning it to coat with oil, and cover with plastic wrap or a clean, damp tea towel. Let the dough rise in a warm spot (I like the oven, turned off but with the light on), until doubled in bulk, about 1 hour.

CONTINUED . . .

CONTINUED...

Or you can make the dough in the morning and let it rise, covered, in the refrigerator during the day.

When you're ready to proceed, divide the dough into 2 to 3 sections. Preheat the oven to 450°F.

Roll the dough out into a rough circle, oval, or rectangle as thin as you like (keep in mind it will rise again in the oven); transfer to a baking sheet or pizza pan sprinkled with flour or cornmeal. Top with your favourite toppings and bake for about 20 minutes, until golden. If you like a crisp bottom crust, halfway through the baking (once the crust is set), slide the pizza off the pan and directly onto one of the oven racks for the last 10 minutes or so. When you're ready to remove it from the oven, slide the pizza back onto the pan or directly onto a cutting board.

**TO MAKE FOCACCIA:**
Follow the directions for pizza dough until the dough has finished its first rise. Preheat the oven to 350°F. Divide the dough into 3 sections and pat each section out to form an 8-inch circle, a little thicker than for a pizza crust. Let it rise until the dough will hold the indent of a finger and not spring back, about 30 minutes. When it's ready to bake, gently prod the top with the tips of your fingers to make shallow divots all across the surface of the dough. Brush or drizzle with a little olive oil; sprinkle with coarse salt and rosemary. Bake for 10 to 15 minutes, until the bread is set, and then slide directly onto one of the oven racks. Continue baking until crisp and golden, another 5 to 10 minutes. Tear into a few rough pieces to serve. Makes 3 focaccia breads, each about 8 inches in diameter.

# WHEAT THINS

MAKES A FAIR OL' SCHWACK OF CRACKERS.

1 cup (250 mL) rinsed and drained canned white beans (half a 19 oz/540 mL can)

¼ cup (60 mL) water

1 cup + 2 Tbsp (280 mL) all-purpose or whole wheat flour, or a combination, plus extra as needed

2 Tbsp (30 mL) olive or canola oil

⅛ tsp (0.5 mL) salt

Coarse salt for sprinkling on top (optional)

A RECIPE THAT doubles easily and will save you a bundle. And you'll look like a deity, but homemade crackers are absurdly easy. Shhh, don't tell anyone. You can fancy these up all you want: a little grated cheese or garlic and rosemary in the dough, cracked pepper or sesame seeds on top.

In the bowl of a food processor, purée the beans and water until smooth. Transfer to a medium bowl and mix in the flour, oil, and salt. Knead once or twice to ensure everything is well combined, adding a little more flour (or water) if necessary to make a smooth dough. Place the dough back in the bowl; cover it and let it rest for about 15 minutes.

Preheat the oven to 325°F. Working with one-quarter of the dough at a time, roll out on a floured surface until very thin, about ¹/₁₆ inch. Sprinkle on the coarse salt (if using) and roll again lightly to help it adhere. Transfer the dough to a dry, floured baking sheet, and repeat with the remaining dough in batches. Everything should fit on 2 large rimmed baking sheets.

Stab the rolled-out dough all over with a fork and use a pizza wheel or knife to cut the sheets into your preferred cracker size. (Ours are usually multi-shaped and all over the place—rustic!) There's no need to separate the crackers, or even cut right to the edge of the sheet—you're really just scoring them.

Bake one sheet at a time for 20 to 30 minutes, depending on how thick the crackers are, until golden and crisp. Transfer to a rack to cool completely, then break apart.

# YEASTED BANANA BREAD
## with Cardamom
### MAKES 1 LARGE BRAIDED LOAF.

¼ cup (60 mL) honey
2 Tbsp (30 mL) butter
1 cup (250 mL) rinsed and
　drained canned white beans
　(half a 19 oz/540 mL can)
2 large, very ripe bananas

1 large egg
2¼ tsp (11 mL) active dry yeast
　(1 package) (see Note)
3½ to 4 cups (875 mL to 1 L)
　all-purpose flour
½ tsp (2.5 mL) salt

¾ tsp (4 mL) ground
　cardamom
1 egg, lightly beaten with 1 tsp
　(5 mL) of water
Coarse sugar, for sprinkling
　(optional)

OLD-WORLD BRAIDED breads seem like a lifetime away for most of us. But if you can braid three strings you can braid bread dough. Best of all, nobody expects neatness—they'll just be blown away that you produced BRAIDED BREAD! This recipe involves a slow rise, which helps both the flavour of the bread and its ability to keep. Leftovers can be sliced and toasted, and topped with peanut butter or chocolate hazelnut spread.

Turn the oven on to its lowest temperature, let it heat for 5 minutes, and then turn it off.

Melt the honey and butter in a small saucepan; let cool briefly. Purée the beans, bananas, and honey mixture in a food processor until combined; add the egg and process until smooth. Transfer to a large bowl, sprinkle the yeast overtop, and stir well.

Add 1 cup of flour to the banana mixture and stir until well combined. Add another cup of flour, the salt, and the cardamom and mix well. Continue adding flour, and when the dough becomes too stiff to continue stirring, turn it out onto a clean countertop and knead it. Keep adding flour until the dough is smooth and not as sticky (though it will still be stickier than a standard yeast dough).

Wash, dry, and lightly oil the bowl. Place the dough in the bowl and turn it to coat with oil. Cover with a clean, damp tea towel and let rise in the oven until the dough is doubled in bulk, about 1½ to 2 hours (but check it earlier, just in case!).

CONTINUED . . .

Baking with Beans

CONTINUED...

When the dough has risen, divide it into 3 pieces. The dough will deflate significantly by itself, but don't hasten or further that—you want it to stay light, not overly compacted. With floured hands, form each piece into a long, thin rope: once you've got it roughly oblong, hold it up and squish it down vertically—like you're trying to squeeze water out of a rope. You'll want each piece to be about 15 inches long. Braid the ropes together, and carefully transfer the bread to a well-buttered baking sheet (or use parchment), tucking the frayed-looking ends under.

Preheat the oven to 350°F about 45 minutes after this point.

**NOTE:**
This recipe does not allow for proofing the yeast before you add other ingredients—therefore make sure you check the best-before date of the yeast you use.

Cover the braid with a piece of parchment paper or oiled plastic wrap and let rise for another 1 to 1½ hours. The dough should yield softly if you press a finger into it, and the indent should remain.

Brush the egg wash over the bread, then sprinkle generously with the coarse sugar (if using). You could use ordinary granulated sugar, though it will dissolve and make things sticky (but still delicious). You can also omit the sugar altogether. Bake the bread for 40 to 45 minutes, until golden. When gently lifted, it should sound hollow when tapped on the bottom. The bread will feel a little heavier than a cooked loaf usually does, and the bottom crust will be quite browned. Cool on a wire rack.

# OATMEAL RAISIN COOKIES

MAKES 1½ TO 2 DOZEN COOKIES.

¼ cup (60 mL) dry red lentils
¼ cup (60 mL) butter, softened
¼ cup (60 mL) canola oil
½ cup (125 mL) packed dark
    brown sugar

½ to 1 tsp (2.5 to 5 mL)
    ground cinnamon
1 large egg
1 tsp (5 mL) vanilla
¾ cup (185 mL) all-purpose
    flour

¾ cup (185 mL) old-fashioned
    or quick oats
½ tsp (2.5 mL) baking soda
½ tsp (2.5 mL) salt
1 cup (250 mL) raisins,
    dried cranberries, or
    chocolate chips

THESE COOKIES ARE wonderful (if we do say so ourselves)—tender, soft, and almost cakey, with a crisp edge. The red lentils fall right into place, cleverly disguising themselves as oats. The combination of butter and canola oil gives these great flavour and less saturated fat than most others. Feel free to swap the raisins for chocolate chips.

Preheat the oven to 350°F.

In a small saucepan, cover the lentils with water and bring to a simmer; cook for 15 minutes, or until soft. Drain well.

In a large bowl, beat the butter, oil, brown sugar, and cinnamon (with an electric mixer or by hand) until creamy; beat in the egg and vanilla.

Add the flour, oats, cooked lentils, baking soda, and salt and stir by hand until almost combined; add the raisins and stir just until blended. Drop large spoonfuls onto a baking sheet that has been sprayed with non-stick cooking spray and bake for 12 to 14 minutes, until set around the edges but still soft in the middle. Transfer to a wire rack to cool.

# PECAN BROWN SUGAR SHORTBREAD

## MAKES 12 WEDGES.

⅓ cup (80 mL) pecans
½ cup (125 mL) butter, divided
½ cup (125 mL) packed brown
   sugar

½ cup (125 mL) rinsed and
   drained canned white beans
¾ cup + 2 Tbsp (215 mL)
   all-purpose or whole

wheat pastry flour,
   or a combination
2 Tbsp (30 mL) cornstarch
Pinch of salt

A VERY SOUTHERN-belle sort of shortbread, which tastes as good as it sounds. It's mostly crumbly, with a thin line of dense chewiness in the middle that's a little reminiscent of butterscotch. Unfortunately we can't tell you how well it keeps, because it's never seen nightfall in either of our houses.

Preheat the oven to 325°F. Spread the pecans on a baking sheet and bake until lightly toasted, about 7 minutes. Remove and allow to cool, then finely grind in a food processor (stop short of making pecan butter). Set aside.

Reserve about 2 Tbsp of butter. Melt the remaining butter in a medium saucepan, then let cool briefly. Process the melted butter, sugar, and beans in a food processor until very smooth. Pour the mixture back into the saucepan and bring to a boil over medium heat, staying attentive and stirring constantly. The mixture will thicken and darken slightly, and after boiling for 5 to 6 minutes it will be sticky and almost gelatinous. Remove from the heat and stir in the reserved butter. Let cool until just warm, about 15 minutes.

In a medium bowl, whisk together the ground pecans, flour, cornstarch, and salt. Add the cooled butter mixture and stir until just combined. Press into an 8- or 9-inch round cake pan and chill until very firm, 1 hour in the freezer or 2 hours in the refrigerator.

Preheat the oven to 325°F. Pierce the cold shortbread all over with the tines of a fork, then bake until set and very palely golden, about 30 minutes. Cut into wedges and let cool completely in the pan.

# CHOCOLATE CRISPS

## MAKES ABOUT 2 DOZEN COOKIES.

¼ cup (60 mL) butter
⅓ cup (80 mL) sugar
½ cup (125 mL) rinsed and
  drained canned white beans

2 Tbsp (30 mL) chopped dark
  chocolate or chocolate chips
¼ cup (60 mL) all-purpose
  flour (yes, ¼ cup—not a
  misprint!)

2 Tbsp (30 mL) unsweetened
  cocoa powder
¼ tsp (1 mL) baking soda
Pinch of salt
1 egg white, lightly beaten

THIN CHOCOLATE wafers—great to have in the lunch bag as insurance against unwise (and oft-regretted) chocolate bar purchases!

Melt the butter in a medium saucepan. Let cool briefly, then process the melted butter, sugar, and beans in a food processor until very smooth. Pour the mixture back into the saucepan and bring to a boil over medium heat, staying attentive and stirring constantly. The mixture will start to thicken and darken slightly, and after boiling for 5 to 6 minutes it will be sticky, reduced in volume, and almost gelatinous. Remove from the heat and let cool for 5 minutes. Stir in the chopped chocolate (it will melt) and allow to cool until just warm, about 10 to 15 minutes.

Preheat the oven to 300°F and set racks in the upper and lower thirds. In a small bowl, stir together the flour, cocoa, baking soda, and salt. Once the sugar and bean mixture is cooled, add the egg white to the saucepan and stir until smooth. Add the flour mixture to the saucepan and stir until just combined; the consistency will be more like thick cake batter than cookie dough. Drop by teaspoonfuls onto 2 baking sheets that have been sprayed with non-stick cooking spray, allowing 2 inches between cookies. Gently pat the dough down with your fingers to flatten, then bake until the edges are crisp and the centres are set, 18 to 20 minutes. Allow to cool on the baking sheet for 2 minutes, then flip upside down and bake for another 5 minutes. Cool completely on a wire rack. The cookies will crisp and harden as they cool.

# GINGER SNAPS

MAKES ABOUT 2 DOZEN COOKIES.

---

¼ cup (60 mL) butter
⅓ cup (80 mL) sugar
½ cup (125 mL) rinsed and
   drained canned white beans
1 Tbsp (15 mL) molasses

⅓ cup (80 mL) flour (yes,
   ⅓ cup—not a misprint!)
2 to 3 tsp (10 to 15 mL) ground
   ginger
1 tsp (5 mL) ground cinnamon

¼ tsp (1 mL) baking soda
Pinch of salt
1 egg white, lightly beaten

---

CLASSIC AND CRISPY—hard! Three teaspoons of ginger will provide a little kick; if you like a lot of kick, add 4 teaspoons, or a big pinch of freshly ground pepper along with it. By boiling the puréed beans with the sugar and butter, you also boil away a lot of moisture, and moisture is the enemy of crispiness—even their fathers didn't get along, nor their fathers' fathers.

Melt the butter in a medium saucepan. Let cool briefly, then process the melted butter, sugar, and beans in a food processor until very smooth. Pour the mixture back into the saucepan and bring to a boil over medium heat, staying attentive and stirring constantly. The mixture will start to thicken and darken slightly, and after boiling for 5 to 6 minutes it will be sticky, reduced in volume, and almost gelatinous. Remove from the heat and let cool for 5 minutes. Stir in the molasses and allow to cool until just warm, about 15 minutes.

Preheat the oven to 300°F and set racks in the upper and lower thirds. In a small bowl, stir together the flour, ginger, cinnamon, baking soda, and salt. Add the egg white to the saucepan with the cooled sugar and bean mixture and stir until smooth. Add the flour mixture and stir until just combined; the consistency will be more like thick cake batter than cookie dough. Drop by teaspoonfuls onto 2 baking sheets that have been sprayed with non-stick cooking spray, allowing 1 inch between cookies. Gently pat the dough down with your fingers to flatten slightly. Bake until the cookies are well set in the middle and lightly browned underneath, about 20 minutes. Allow to cool on the baking sheet for 2 minutes, then flip upside down and bake for another 10 minutes. Cool completely on a wire rack. The cookies will crisp and harden as they cool.

# GINGER CHEWS
## MAKES ABOUT 1½ DOZEN COOKIES.

¼ cup (60 mL) butter
½ cup (125 mL) sugar
½ cup (125 mL) rinsed and
   drained canned white beans

1 Tbsp (15 mL) molasses
¼ cup (60 mL) flour (we say
   again: ¼ cup)
2 tsp (10 mL) ground ginger

1 tsp (5 mL) ground cinnamon
¼ tsp (1 mL) baking soda
Pinch of salt
1 large egg white, lightly beaten

THESE COOKIES ARE very thin and chewy, and altogether addictive. The batter spreads a lot, so be sure to use only the teaspoon of batter specified, and leave plenty of space between cookies.

Melt the butter in a medium saucepan (you'll be putting everything into it shortly) and let cool briefly. Pour the butter into the bowl of a food processor, add the sugar and beans, and process until very smooth, scraping down the bowl once or twice. Pour the contents back into the unwashed saucepan and cook over medium heat until the mixture boils. You'll want to stay attentive and stir constantly. The mixture will start to thicken and darken slightly, and in about 5 to 6 minutes from the time it's boiled it will be sticky and reduced in volume, and almost gelatinous in texture. Remove the pan from the heat, stir in the molasses, and allow to cool until just warm, about 20 minutes (quicker in the refrigerator, but watch the glass shelves!).

Preheat the oven to 325°F and set racks in the upper and lower thirds. In a small bowl, stir together the flour, ginger, cinnamon, baking soda, and salt. Once the sugar and bean mixture is cooled, add the egg white to the pot and stir until smooth. Add the flour mixture to the pot and stir until just combined; the consistency will be more like cake batter than cookie dough.

Drop by teaspoonfuls onto 2 baking sheets that have been sprayed with non-stick cooking spray, allowing 2 inches between cookies. Bake for 10 to 12 minutes, until lightly browned at the edges and just set in the middle. Let cool on the sheet for a couple minutes, and then transfer to a wire rack to finish cooling.

# BLACK BEAN BROWNIES

## MAKES 16 BROWNIES.

1 cup (250 mL) rinsed and drained canned black beans (half a 19 oz/540 mL can)

1¼ cups (310 mL) broken pecan pieces (optional)

½ cup (125 mL) butter

2 oz (60 g) unsweetened chocolate

⅓ cup (80 mL) all-purpose flour

Pinch of salt

2 large eggs

¾ cup (185 mL) sugar

1 tsp (5 mL) vanilla

⅔ cup (160 mL) good-quality chocolate chips, or a 3½ oz (100 g) bar good quality bittersweet or semi-sweet dark chocolate, chopped

THESE ARE THE FULL-on real deal. Nobody has ever detected the merest hint of a bean in these, nor given a damn once told. Use good-quality chocolate; you'll be happy you did.

Preheat the oven to 350°F.

Spread the rinsed black beans out on a double thickness of paper towel and blot them gently to remove as much moisture as possible. Leave them uncovered on the counter until you need them for the recipe.

Spread the pecan pieces (if using) on a rimmed baking sheet and toast in the oven until fragrant and very lightly browned, about 6 to 7 minutes. Set aside to cool.

In a small saucepan set over very low heat, melt the butter and unsweetened chocolate, taking care not to let the mixture scorch. Whisk to combine, then remove from the heat and let cool for a few minutes. In a medium bowl, whisk the flour and salt together and set aside.

Place the dried-off beans and the cooled butter/chocolate mixture in the bowl of a food processor, and process until very smooth, scraping down the bowl once or twice. Add the eggs, sugar, and vanilla; process again until combined. Scrape the mixture into the flour mixture and fold gently,

CONTINUED . . .

CONTINUED . . . leaving streaks of flour still visible. Add the pecans and chocolate chips and fold to just combine.

Pour the batter into a lightly buttered (or sprayed, with non-stick cooking spray) 8-inch square pan, and smooth the top. Bake for 28 to 30 minutes: the batter should no longer jiggle when the pan moves, but any toothpick inserted would be very chocolatey indeed. Let cool completely in the pan on a wire rack. The brownies will need to cool awhile, unless you want to eat them with a spoon directly from the pan (we've done it). Otherwise, cut them when they've cooled, and store in the refrigerator if you like a dense texture, or at room temperature if you like them softer.

# FOUR SEASONS OF FRUIT CRISP

SERVES 6–8.

**SPRING FILLING:**

1¼ lb (625 g) rhubarb, stalks trimmed and cut into ½-inch pieces

1 lb (500 g) strawberries, hulled and halved or quartered, depending on their size

¾ cup (185 mL) sugar

3 to 4 Tbsp (45 to 60 mL) cornstarch (use the higher amount for really juicy strawberries—locally grown if you're lucky!)

**EARLY SUMMER FILLING:**

2½ lb (1.25 kg) dark cherries such as Bing or Vans, pitted

½ tsp (2.5 mL) almond extract (optional)

⅓ cup (80 mL) sugar

2 Tbsp (30 mL) cornstarch

**LATER SUMMER FILLING:**

4 lb (1.8 kg) ripe peaches, peeled (see Note on page 249), pitted, and sliced

⅓ cup (80 mL) sugar

3 to 4 Tbsp (45 to 60 mL) cornstarch (use the higher amount for very juicy peaches)

1 tsp (5 mL) ground cinnamon (optional)

**AUTUMN FILLING:**

3 lb (1.5 kg) Italian prune plums, halved and pitted

1 Tbsp (15 mL) vanilla

¾ cup (185 mL) sugar

3 Tbsp (45 mL) cornstarch

**WINTER FILLING:**

4 to 5 apples or pears (or a combination), peeled if you like, cored, and sliced

½ cup (125 mL) fresh or frozen cranberries

Grated zest of 1 orange or 1 lemon, to be mixed in with the fruit

⅓ cup (80 mL) sugar

1 Tbsp (15 mL) cornstarch

½ tsp (2.5 mL) ground cinnamon

**TOPPING:**

⅔ cup (160 mL) Candied Red Lentils (page 259) or Candied Lentil Meal (page 260)

1 cup (250 mL) oats, old-fashioned or quick-cooking (not instant)

½ cup (125 mL) all-purpose or whole wheat flour

⅓ cup (80 mL) packed brown sugar

⅓ cup (80 mL) butter, softened

CONTINUED . . .

CONTINUED ...

FRUIT CRISPS ARE TOP-DRAWER DESSERTS: ALL flavour and no pretension. They're also extremely adaptable; you can get the best of the season's fresh produce to the table, or just use up whatever you have in the refrigerator or freezer.

In all cases you can assume that the sugar called for in the fillings will yield a slightly tart result, but will still be definitely dessert-like. If you prefer things really tart, reduce the sugar slightly, or if you like things quite sweet, you'll want to increase it slightly.

On baking dishes: a glass or ceramic dish is preferable for crisps, but metal is OK, too; you just don't want to store the crisp in a metal dish for very long, as the acidity of the fruit can alter the finish of a metal dish and give the fruit a metallic taste. These recipes use either a deep dish pie plate measuring 8 inches across the bottom, or an 8-inch square glass dish, 2 inches deep. When you first add the fruit to the dish, it will come nearly level with the rim, but as the fruit cooks down there will be room for the topping, too. It's a good idea to set the dish on a pizza pan or baking sheet as insurance against spills.

It hardly needs saying, but use these fillings as a place to start. Use whatever fruit is available: blueberries, raspberries, apricots, saskatoon berries, etc., and combine however you like. You can also add chopped or ground nuts to the topping, or a pinch or two of cinnamon.

Preheat the oven to 400°F. Place the prepared fruit in a large bowl. For cherry or plum fillings, toss well with the vanilla or almond extract (if using). In a small bowl, combine the sugar and cornstarch (and cinnamon if it's called for), add to the fruit, and toss well to combine. Tip into a lightly buttered baking dish and bake, gently stirring once or twice, until the fruit has released its juice and is hot but not yet cooked through, about 20 to 25 minutes. Stir gently, redistributing the fruit in the dish to ensure the hotter bits at the edge get into the middle and vice-versa. This step helps the fruit cook more evenly.

Reduce the oven temperature to 350°F. In a medium bowl, combine the lentils, oats, flour, and brown sugar. Using a pastry blender or your fingers, work the butter into the dry ingredients until the mixture is crumbly. Add the crisp topping to the partially baked filling, squeezing handfuls of the topping to compact it slightly, and distributing it over the filling. The end result should be slightly piled up, and with plenty of gaps where the filling is visible beneath the crumbs—this will allow the juices to release their steam into the oven, and will better allow the filling to thicken. Return to the oven and bake until the fruit juices are bubbling thickly around the edges and about halfway to the centre, and the topping is starting to colour, about 30 to 40 minutes. If the topping is browning too quickly, lay tin foil loosely overtop of the crisp.

**NOTE:**

To peel peaches, drop them into a saucepan of boiling water for a minute or two, then plunge them into ice water. You should now be able to slip the skins off easily (be warned, it's still messy: might want to change out of the Vera Wang).

# THICK, CHEWY GRANOLA BARS
### MAKES 12 TO 16 PIECES.

1¾ cups (435 mL) old-fashioned or quick-cooking oats, barley flakes, or a combination

½ cup (125 mL) packed brown sugar

⅓ cup (80 mL) oat or quinoa flour (or finely ground oats)

½ tsp (2.5 mL) salt

¼ tsp (1 mL) ground cinnamon (optional)

2 cups (500 mL) chopped mixed dried fruit, nuts, and seeds

1 cup (250 mL) Candied Red Lentils (page 259)

⅓ cup (80 mL) canola oil

⅓ cup (80 mL) peanut butter or golden pea butter

⅓ cup (80 mL) liquid honey, maple syrup, or corn syrup

2 tsp (10 mL) vanilla

GRANOLA BARS ARE SO much better made from scratch, and can be customized with any nuts, seeds, and dried fruit your kids like, in any proportion. Golden pea butter is available across Canada and in parts of the US and is well worth seeking out, but peanut or any other nut butter works as well. If you don't have oat flour, make some by processing oats in a food processor until powdery, or try substituting brown rice or quinoa flour, which is available at most health food stores.

Preheat the oven to 350°F and spray an 8- or 9-inch square pan with non-stick cooking spray.

In a large bowl, stir together the oats, brown sugar, oat flour, salt, and cinnamon (if using). Stir in the dried fruit, nuts, seeds, and lentils.

In a small bowl, whisk together the canola oil, peanut butter, honey, and vanilla. Add to the dry ingredients and stir until well blended and crumbly. Press into the prepared pan.

Bake for 30 to 35 minutes, until golden around the edges. Cool completely in the pan on a wire rack before cutting into squares or bars.

# BAKLAVA

MAKES 48 PIECES.

1 package (1 lb/500 g) phyllo
    pastry, thawed
3 cups (750 mL) walnuts,
    chopped
1 cup (250 mL) Candied Red
    Lentils (see page 259)

⅓ cup (80 mL) sugar
1 tsp (5 mL) ground cinnamon
½ tsp (2.5 mL) ground
    cardamom (optional)
½ cup (125 mL) butter,
    melted

**SYRUP:**
2 cups (500 mL) sugar
1 cup (250 mL) water
½ cup (125 mL) honey
Thick strip of lemon peel (cut
    a slice off with a vegetable
    peeler, getting mostly the
    outer yellow part)

MULTI-LAYERED baklava might sound daunting, but is actually a snap to make. It's great when you have to feed a large group of people—a panful will give you almost 50 pieces. When working with phyllo, remember that it's very forgiving—because there are so many layers, you don't have to worry about it being perfectly straight, or whether it cracks or tears. As long as the one on top is intact, your baklava will be perfection.

Preheat the oven to 375°F. In a small bowl, stir together the walnuts, candied lentils, sugar, and spices.

Make sure your phyllo is completely thawed, and keep the sheets covered with a tea towel or piece of plastic wrap to keep them from drying out. Place 2 sheets of phyllo on the bottom of a rimmed baking pan or jelly roll pan (about 12 × 16 inches) and brush lightly with butter. Add 3 more stacks of 2 sheets (it's easier to pull them off the pile 2 at a time), brushing with butter between each stack. Once you have 8 pieces of phyllo, spread one-third of the nut mixture overtop.

Place 4 more sheets of phyllo on top of the nuts, brushing melted butter between each sheet or every 2 sheets. Repeat with another third of the nut mixture, another 4 sheets (brushing with butter as above), and the rest of the nuts. Layer the remaining sheets of phyllo on top of the nuts in the same way; brush the top sheet with butter as well. Tuck in any sticking-out edges.

Cut the pastry lengthwise into 4 strips, then crosswise into 6, making 24 pieces (they don't have to be square), being sure not to slice through the bottom layer of phyllo. (This allows the syrup to soak in better.) Make diagonal cuts through each piece, making them triangles (you'll end up with 48).

Bake for 20 to 25 minutes, or until golden. While the baklava bakes, combine the sugar, water, honey, and lemon peel in a pan set over medium-high heat and bring to a boil. Remove from the heat and take out the lemon peel.

When the baklava comes out of the oven, immediately pour the hot syrup evenly overtop. Let the baklava stand at room temperature until completely cool. Slice through each piece completely before serving.

# UPSIDE-DOWN PEAR GINGERBREAD
## SERVES 8.

**TOPPING:**

1 Tbsp (15 mL) butter

2 Tbsp (30 mL) honey

⅓ cup (80 mL) packed
   brown sugar

1 or 2 firm but ripe pears
   or tart apples, peeled
   and sliced thinly

**GINGERBREAD:**

¼ cup (60 mL) butter

½ cup (125 mL) packed
   brown sugar

1 large egg

¼ cup (60 mL) buttermilk
   or sour milk

½ cup (125 mL) rinsed and
   drained canned white beans

¼ cup (60 mL) molasses

1 Tbsp (15 mL) grated fresh
   ginger, or 1 tsp (5 mL)
   ground ginger

¾ cup (185 mL) all-purpose
   flour

1 tsp (5 mL) baking soda

½ tsp (2.5 mL) ground
   cinnamon

¼ tsp (1 mL) ground allspice
   (optional)

¼ tsp (1 mL) salt

PEARS AND GINGER
were made for each other—
add a sweetly moist cake
and all you need is a scoop
of vanilla ice cream or
barely sweetened whipped
cream. Or you can side
it with yogurt and call
it breakfast—yahoo!

Preheat the oven to 350°F and spray an 8- or 9-inch round cake pan with non-stick cooking spray.

TO MAKE THE TOPPING: Combine the butter, honey, and brown sugar in a small saucepan over medium heat and stir until smooth. Spread evenly over the bottom of the cake pan, then lay the pear slices overtop, keeping them tight together or even very slightly overlapping. Set aside.

TO MAKE THE GINGERBREAD: Beat the butter and sugar together in a medium bowl until smooth and fluffy, add the egg, and beat well again. Process the buttermilk, beans, and molasses in a food processor until smooth, and stir into the butter mixture along with the fresh ginger, if you're using it—otherwise, ground ginger goes in with the

dry ingredients. In a small bowl, combine the flour, baking soda, cinnamon, allspice (if using), and salt. Add the dry ingredients to the butter mixture and stir gently until just combined; be careful not to overmix. Smooth the batter over the sliced pears.

Bake the gingerbread for 35 to 40 minutes, until a tester inserted in the centre comes out clean. Let cool for 5 minutes or so, then invert a serving plate over the cake pan. Quickly but carefully flip both upside down, and let the cake pan rest on top of the plate for a moment or two. Remove the cake pan. If you have any pear slices stuck in the pan, just peel them off and place them on the cake—you'll see where they belong.

# APRICOT-ALMOND
## *Biscotti*

### MAKES ABOUT 2 DOZEN BISCOTTI.

1¾ cups (435 mL) all-purpose flour, or a combination of all-purpose and whole wheat
1 cup (250 mL) oats, old-fashioned or quick-cooking
¾ cup (185 mL) sugar (white or brown)
1 tsp (5 mL) baking powder
¼ tsp (1 mL) salt

¼ cup (60 mL) butter
1 cup (250 mL) rinsed and drained canned white beans (half a 19 oz/540 mL can)
¼ cup (60 mL) orange juice or milk
¼ cup (60 mL) canola oil
1 large egg

2 tsp (10 mL) vanilla (or any flavoured extract)
½ to 1 cup (125 to 250 mL) sliced or slivered almonds
½ cup (125 mL) chopped dried apricots
Coarse sugar, for sprinkling (optional)

THIS BISCOTTI IS crisp without being hard on the teeth; if you prefer it soft, bake the log of dough only once, then slice and serve it without the second baking. (It is, after all, baked through at that point.) Use this as a basic canvas for any type of biscotti you want to make—grate orange or lemon zest into the bean mixture to flavour the dough, or add cinnamon or other spices to the dry ingredients. Beyond that, add nuts, seeds, chopped chocolate, dried fruit—use your imagination.

Preheat the oven to 350°F. In the bowl of a food processor, combine the flour, oats, sugar, baking powder, and salt; pulse until the oats are finely ground. Add the butter and pulse to blend. Transfer the mixture to a large bowl.

Put the beans, juice, oil, egg, and vanilla into the food processor and pulse until smooth; add to the dry ingredients along with the almonds and apricots. Stir until combined.

Shape the dough into a log on a baking sheet sprayed with non-stick cooking spray (it will be a bit sticky—dampening your hands helps), flattening it so that it's about 15 inches long and 4 inches wide. If you like, sprinkle the top with coarse sugar.

Bake for 25 to 30 minutes, until golden and firm. Transfer to a wire rack to cool, then cut on a slight diagonal into ½-inch-thick slices using a serrated knife. Stand the biscotti upright on the baking sheet, spacing them about ½ inch apart, and bake for another 30 minutes, until crisp and dry.

# RED LENTIL PUMPKIN PIE

## MAKES 1 PIE.

⅓ cup (80 mL) dry red lentils

14 oz (398 mL) can puréed pumpkin

¾ cup (185 mL) half-and-half, evaporated 2% milk, or whipping cream

½ cup (125 mL) sugar

½ cup (125 mL) packed brown sugar

3 large eggs

1 Tbsp (15 mL) molasses (optional)

1 Tbsp (15 mL) grated fresh ginger, or ½ tsp (2.5 mL) ground ginger

1 tsp (5 mL) vanilla

1 tsp (5 mL) ground cinnamon, or more to taste

¼ tsp (1 mL) ground allspice

Pinch of salt

1 unbaked 9-inch pie shell

YES, WE REALIZE THAT the title might not appeal to everyone—make sure when you bring it ceremoniously to the table that you refer to it only as "pumpkin pie." No one will be able to detect red lentils in it. We like to cut the trimmed scraps of pastry into tiny leaves, with "veins" made gently with the tip of a sharp knife, bake them separately on a cookie sheet, and then lay them on top of the baked pie. We're channelling our inner Marthas.

In a small saucepan, cover the lentils with water and bring to a boil; cook for 20 minutes, or until very soft. Drain. Preheat the oven to 350°F.

Put the lentils into the bowl of a food processor with the remaining ingredients (except the crust, of course) and pulse until well blended and smooth. Pour into the crust.

Bake for 50 to 60 minutes, until the filling is set but still just a little wobbly in the middle, and the crust is golden. If the crust is browning too quickly, cover the pie lightly with a sheet of tin foil as it bakes. Cool completely in the pan on a wire rack. Serve at room temperature with whipped cream sweetened with a little sugar or maple syrup and spiked with a few drops of vanilla.

# CANDIED RED LENTILS
## and Lentil Meal

MAKES A LITTLE LESS THAN 2 CUPS.

| | | |
|---|---|---|
| 1 cup (250 mL) red lentils | 1¾ cups (435 mL) water<br>¼ cup (60 mL) butter | ½ cup (125 mL) packed<br>brown sugar |

THESE CANDIED lentils can be used in so many ways: you can add them to muffins, crisp toppings, cookies—whatever you might add nuts and seeds to. The red lentils really lend themselves to this preparation; when boiled with the sugar and butter they retain their shape to a much greater degree than usual, and their colour is appealing in most baked goods. The lentil meal is the more disguisable of the two, so if you need to be sneaky, we suggest you start there. The flavour of the lentil meal is quite reminiscent of graham cracker crumbs— nothing scary or hard-core. We eat them straight up.

In a medium saucepan, bring the lentils and water to a boil. Boil until the lentils are partially cooked but not yet losing their shape, 10 to 12 minutes. Stir in the butter and sugar and reduce the heat a little. Cook, partially covered, until the lentils are tender and have taken on the flavour of the sugar and butter, adding a little more water if things are getting too dry. Turn off the heat and let the lentils cool in the pot—they'll continue to absorb liquid as they cool.

Preheat the oven to 350°F.

Spread the cooled lentils over a large parchment-lined rimmed baking sheet. Bake, stirring and re-spreading the lentils once or twice, for 30 minutes. Turn the oven down to 300°F, and continue baking (and stirring occasionally) until they turn a shade or two darker and are starting to crisp up, another 20 to 30 minutes. The lentils will continue to dry out after they're cooled. Store in an airtight container for several days, or freeze for longer storage.

CONTINUED . . .

CONTINUED . . .

### CANDIED LENTIL MEAL
Preheat the oven to 350°F.

Cook the lentils in a medium saucepan with enough water to cover until soft, 15 to 20 minutes. Drain and let cool briefly, then place in the bowl of a food processor. Add the butter and brown sugar; the butter will melt, but it's OK— it's all part of the plan! Process until smooth, and don't be alarmed at the unattractive colour and . . . er . . . texture (and try not to make any crude jokes!)—things will look more appealing shortly.

Spread the paste evenly on a large parchment-lined rimmed baking sheet, and bake for 20 minutes, stirring once and re-spreading the paste. Turn the oven down to 300°F, and bake for another 20 to 30 minutes. The edges will start to brown and crisp long before the centre does; be sure to mix the paste around about every 10 minutes so things progress as evenly as possible. The paste will turn into damp crumbles, and you'll want to break up the clumps after stirring. When the mixture is dry and crumbly, and toasted in places, remove from the oven and let cool completely. Process again in the food processor to break up the clumps, and then spread the meal back out on the parchment to dry completely. Store in an airtight container for several days, or freeze for longer storage.

# INDEX

**A**

Aloo Gobi with Chickpeas · 148
amino acids · 2, 3, 7
Antipasto · 49
appetizers and dips
  *Antipasto · 49*
  *Cheesy Black Bean Dip · 50*
  *Curried Dal Dip · 44*
  *Edamame or Broad Bean & Walnut*
    *Dip · 45*
  *Hoisin Black Bean Lettuce Wraps · 52*
  *Hummus Five Ways · 40*
  *Marinated Roasted Eggplant, Pepper &*
    *Mushrooms with Lentils · 54*
  *Samosas · 42*
  *Savoury Hand Pies with Sun-Dried*
    *Tomatoes, Lentils, Olives &*
    *Feta · 58*
  *Spiced Roasted Chickpeas with*
    *Walnuts · 47*
  *Spinach & Artichoke Dip with White*
    *Beans · 60*
  *Vietnamese Rice Paper Rolls · 62*
  *White Bean, Tomato & Olive*
    *Bruschetta · 57*
apples
  *Apple, Sprouted Bean & Crystalized*
    *Ginger Salad with Cambozola · 80*
  *Turkey & Black Bean Chili with*
    *Butternut Squash & Apples · 175*
Apricot-Almond Biscotti · 257
artichoke
  *Spinach and Artichoke Dip with White*
    *Beans · 60*
asparagus
  *Stir-Fried Chickpeas & Asparagus*
    *with Brown Rice & Lemon Tahini*
    *Dressing · 169*
avocado
  *Sausage & Chickpea Soup with Garlic &*
    *Avocado · 128*

**B**

bacon
  *Poached Eggs over Warm Lentils with*
    *Bacon · 167*
  *Roasted Chickpeas & Pecans with Bacon*
    *& Maple Syrup · 32*
baked beans
  *Guinness Baked Beans · 201*
  *Maple Baked Beans · 202*
Baked Mac & Cheese with Little
  White Beans · 184
Baked Penne with Sausage,
  Spinach & Beans · 187
baking with beans
  *about · 210*
  *Apricot-Almond Biscotti · 257*
  *Baklava · 252*
  *Banana Bread · 216*
  *Black Bean Brownies · 244*
  *Blueberry Big Crumb Cake · 220*
  *Brioche Burger or Slider Buns · 224*
  *Candied Red Lentils and Lentil*
    *Meal · 260*
  *Carrot Cake · 222*
  *Chocolate Crisps · 240*
  *Chocolate Cupcakes · 211*
  *Citrus Bliss Pound Cake · 218*
  *Four Seasons of Fruit Crisp · 247*
  *Ginger Chews · 242*
  *Ginger Snaps · 241*
  *Naan · 223*
  *No-Knead Bread · 226*
  *Oatmeal Raisin Cookies · 237*
  *Oatmeal Raisin Scones · 212*
  *Pecan Brown Sugar Shortbread · 238*
  *Pizza Dough (& Focaccia) · 230*
  *Pretzels · 229*
  *Pumpkin Chocolate Chip Loaf*
    *Cake · 215*
  *Red Lentil Pumpkin Pie · 258*
  *Thick, Chewy Granola Bars · 250*

*Upside-Down Pear Gingerbread · 254*
  *Wheat Thins · 233*
  *Yeasted Banana Bread with*
    *Cardamom · 234*
  *Zucchini Bread · 217*
Baklava · 252
bananas
  *Banana Bread · 216*
  *Yeasted Banana Bread with*
    *Cardamom · 234*
barley
  *about · 10*
  *Barley & Wheat Berry Salad with*
    *Chickpeas & Feta · 69*
  *Beef & Barley Chili · 158*
  *Brown & Wild Rice & Barley Salad with*
    *Chickpeas · 72*
  *Charred Corn, Black Bean & Toasted*
    *Barley Salad · 76*
  *Lentil & Barley Salad with Tomatoes,*
    *Spinach & Feta · 71*
  *Sausage, Lentil & Barley Soup · 138*
  *Tabbouleh with Barley &*
    *Chickpeas · 90*
bean sprouts *see* sprouted beans
beans (general) *see* legumes
beany sides
  *Chard, White Bean & Sweet Potato*
    *Gratin · 205*
  *Easy Red Lentil Dal · 207*
  *Guinness Baked Beans · 201*
  *Lentils Braised in Red Wine · 206*
  *Maple Baked Beans · 202*
  *Roasted Chickpeas with Garlic &*
    *Chard · 200*
  *White Bean Mashed Potatoes · 203*
Beef & Barley Chili · 158
beets
  *Beet & Black Bean Burgers · 101*
  *Roasted Beet Salad with Wild Rice,*
    *Goat Cheese & Chickpeas · 87*

biscotti
  Apricot–Almond Biscotti · 257
black beans
  Beet & Black Bean Burgers · 101
  Black Bean Breakfast Burritos · 27
  Black Bean Brownies · 244
  Black Bean Quesadillas · 100
  Black Bean Soup · 112
  Charred Corn, Black Bean & Toasted
    Barley Salad · 76
  Cheesy Black Bean Dip · 50
  Chorizo, Black Bean & Corn
    Chowder · 131
  Crispy Black Bean Tacos with Feta &
    Slaw · 98
  Curried Quinoa Salad with Black Beans
    & Mango · 66
  Hoisin Black Bean Lettuce Wraps · 52
  Mexican Fried Rice · 160
  Roasted Red Pepper, Tomato & Black
    Bean Soup · 134
  Sunny Side Up Breakfast Pizzas · 29
  Sausage, Black Bean & Sweet Potato
    Soup · 135
  Thai Chicken Thighs with Black Beans
    & Sweet Potatoes · 173
  Turkey & Black Bean Chili with
    Butternut Squash & Apples · 175
  Two–Bean & Sweet Potato Chipotle
    Chili · 159
black-eyed peas
  Black-Eyed Pea & Kale Soup with
    Cheesy Croutons · 126
  Spaghetti Cacio e Pepe e Fagioli · 194
Blueberry Big Crumb Cake · 220
breads (quick) see cakes and muffins
breads (yeast)
  Brioche Burger or Slider Buns · 224
  Naan · 223
  No-Knead Bread · 226
  Pizza Dough (& Focaccia) · 230
  Sticky Cinnamon Buns · 24
  Yeasted Banana Bread with
    Cardamom · 234
breakfast
  Black Bean Breakfast Burritos · 27
  Buttermilk Waffles · 18
  Cranberry Cornmeal Mini
    Muffins · 23
  Granola · 37
  Huevos Rancheros · 30
  Morning Glory Muffins · 20

  Pancakes · 16
  Roasted Chickpeas & Pecans with
    Bacon & Maple Syrup · 32
  Spanish Tortilla with Lentils · 35
  Sticky Cinnamon Buns · 24
  Sunny Side Up Breakfast Pizzas · 29
Brioche Burger or Slider
  Buns · 224
broad beans
  Edamame or Broad Bean & Walnut
    Dip · 45
Brown & Wild Rice & Barley
  Salad with Chickpeas · 72
Brown Rice Pasta with Mush-
  rooms, Prosciutto &
  Sprouted Beans · 193
brown sugar
  Pecan Brown Sugar Shortbread · 238
brownies
  Black Bean Brownies · 244
bruschetta
  White Bean, Tomato & Olive
    Bruschetta · 57
buckwheat · 12
bulgur · 11
burgers see sandwiches
burritos
  Black Bean Breakfast Burritos · 27
Butter Chicken & Lentils · 176
Buttermilk Waffles · 18

C

cakes
  Banana Bread · 216
  Blueberry Big Crumb Cake · 220
  Carrot Cake · 222
  Chocolate Cupcakes · 211
  Citrus Bliss Pound Cake · 218
  Pumpkin Chocolate Chip Loaf
    Cake · 215
  Upside-Down Pear Gingerbread · 254
  Zucchini Bread · 217
cambozola
  Apple, Sprouted Bean & Crystalized
    Ginger Salad with Cambozola · 80
Candied Red Lentils and Lentil
  Meal · 259
capers, fried · 181
cardamom
  Yeasted Banana Bread with
    Cardamom · 234

carrots
  Carrot Cake · 222
  Curried Sweet Potato, Carrot & Red
    Lentil Soup · 132
cauliflower
  Aloo Gobi with Chickpeas · 148
  Quinoa, Cauliflower, Chickpea & Feta
    Sort-of-Slaw · 74
Chana Masala · 145
chard
  Chard, White Bean & Sweet Potato
    Gratin · 205
  Lebanese Spinach & Lentil Soup · 118
  Roasted Chickpeas with Garlic &
    Chard · 200
  Spaghetti with Garlic, Chickpeas &
    Braised Kale or Chard · 191
Charred Corn, Black Bean &
  Toasted Barley Salad · 76
cheddar
  Baked Mac & Cheese with Little White
    Beans · 184
  Cheesy Black Bean Dip · 50
  Chicken, White Bean, Corn & Cheddar
    Chowder · 130
cheese see also specific cheeses
  Chard, White Bean & Sweet Potato
    Gratin · 205
  Spaghetti Cacio e Pepe e Fagioli · 194
Cheesy Black Bean Dip · 50
chicken
  Butter Chicken & Lentils · 176
  Chicken & Bean Braise · 180
  Chicken & White Bean Stew with
    Pesto · 139
  Chicken Noodle Soup · 110
  Chicken, White Bean, Corn & Cheddar
    Chowder · 130
  Thai Chicken Thighs with Black Beans
    & Sweet Potatoes · 173
chickpeas
  Aloo Gobi with Chickpeas · 148
  Barley & Wheat Berry Salad with
    Chickpeas & Feta · 69
  Brown & Wild Rice & Barley Salad
    with Chickpeas · 72
  Chana Masala · 145
  Chickpea Masala Sandwiches
    (Doubles) · 106
  Classic Three-Bean Salad · 79
  Couscous with Roasted Vegetables, Feta
    & Chickpeas · 152

Index

*Falafel · 96*
*Greek Salad with Chickpeas &*
  *Bow-Ties · 84*
*Hummus Five Ways · 40*
*Italian Vegetable Stew · 116*
*Mulligatawny Soup · 115*
*Quick Chickpea Curry · 147*
*Quinoa, Cauliflower, Chickpea & Feta*
  *Sort-of-Slaw · 74*
*Rice or Orzo Salad with Chickpeas,*
  *Spinach, Lemon & Feta · 78*
*Roasted Beet Salad with Wild Rice,*
  *Goat Cheese & Chickpeas · 87*
*Roasted Chickpeas & Pecans with Bacon*
  *& Maple Syrup · 32*
*Roasted Chickpeas with Garlic &*
  *Chard · 200*
*Samosas · 42*
*Sausage & Chickpea Soup with Garlic &*
  *Avocado · 128*
*Spaghetti with Garlic, Chickpeas &*
  *Braised Kale or Chard · 191*
*Spiced Couscous Salad with*
  *Chickpeas · 88*
*Spiced Roasted Chickpeas with*
  *Walnuts · 47*
*Stir-Fried Chickpeas & Asparagus*
  *with Brown Rice & Lemon Tahini*
  *Dressing · 169*
*Tabbouleh with Barley &*
  *Chickpeas · 90*
*Turkey Chickpea Sliders · 104*
chili
  *Beef & Barley Chili · 158*
  *Turkey & Black Bean Chili with*
    *Butternut Squash & Apples · 175*
  *Two-Bean & Sweet Potato Chipotle*
    *Chili · 159*
chocolate
  *Chocolate Crisps · 240*
  *Chocolate Cupcakes · 211*
  *Pumpkin Chocolate Chip Loaf*
    *Cake · 215*
Chorizo, Black Bean & Corn
  Chowder · 131
cinnamon buns
  *Sticky Cinnamon Buns · 24*
Citrus Bliss Pound Cake · 218
Classic Three-Bean Salad · 79
Coconut Dal Curry · 151
Cold Soba Noodles with Miso
  Dressing · 83

cookies
  *Chocolate Crisps · 240*
  *Ginger Chews · 242*
  *Ginger Snaps · 241*
  *Oatmeal Raisin Cookies · 237*
  *Pecan Brown Sugar Shortbread · 238*
corn
  *Charred Corn, Black Bean & Toasted*
    *Barley Salad · 76*
  *Chicken, White Bean, Corn & Cheddar*
    *Chowder · 130*
  *Chorizo, Black Bean & Corn Chowder · 131*
cornmeal
  *Cranberry Cornmeal Mini Muffins · 23*
couscous
  *about · 11*
  *Couscous with Roasted Vegetables, Feta*
    *& Chickpeas · 152*
  *Marinated Lentil Couscous Salad · 73*
  *Spiced Couscous Salad with*
    *Chickpeas · 88*
crackers
  *Wheat Thins · 233*
Cranberry Cornmeal Mini
  Muffins · 23
cream sauce
  *Soba Noodles with Mushroom & Lentil*
    *Cream Sauce · 192*
Creamy Mushroom Soup with
  Little White Beans · 113
crisp
  *Four Seasons of Fruit Crisp · 247*
Crispy Black Bean Tacos with
  Feta & Slaw · 98
croutons
  *Black-Eyed Pea & Kale Soup with*
    *Cheesy Croutons · 126*
curry
  *Coconut Dal Curry · 151*
  *Curried Dal Dip · 44*
  *Curried Quinoa Salad with Black Beans*
    *& Mango · 66*
  *Curried Sweet Potato, Carrot & Red*
    *Lentil Soup · 132*
  *Quick Chickpea Curry · 147*
  *Red Lentil & Sweet Potato Curry with*
    *Spinach · 146*
  *Vegetable Lentil Curry · 150*

**D**
dal
  *Coconut Dal Curry · 151*
  *Curried Dal Dip · 44*
  *Easy Red Lentil Dal · 207*
  *Palak Dal · 179*
dips *see* appetizers and dips
doubles
  *Chickpea Masala Sandwiches*
    *(Doubles) · 106*

**E**
Easy Red Lentil Dal · 207
Edamame or Broad Bean &
  Walnut Dip · 45
eggplant
  *Marinated Roasted Eggplant, Pepper &*
    *Mushroom with Lentils · 54*
eggs
  *Black Bean Breakfast Burritos · 27*
  *Huevos Rancheros · 30*
  *Poached Eggs over Warm Lentils with*
    *Bacon · 167*
  *Spanish Tortilla with Lentils · 35*
  *Sunny Side Up Breakfast Pizzas · 29*

**F**
Falafel · 96
feta
  *Barley & Wheat Berry Salad with*
    *Chickpeas & Feta · 69*
  *Couscous with Roasted Vegetables, Feta*
    *& Chickpeas · 152*
  *Crispy Black Bean Tacos with Feta*
    *& Slaw · 98*
  *Lentil & Barley Salad with Tomatoes,*
    *Spinach & Feta · 71*
  *Quinoa, Cauliflower, Chickpea & Feta*
    *Sort-of-Slaw · 74*
  *Rice or Orzo Salad with Chickpeas,*
    *Spinach, Lemon & Feta · 78*
  *Savoury Hand Pies with Sun-Dried*
    *Tomatoes, Lentils, Olives &*
    *Feta · 58*
fish
  *New-School Tuna Melts · 105*
  *Seafood Chowder · 125*
  *White Bean & Tuna Pasta Salad · 92*
flatulence · 3, 6
focaccia
  *Pizza Dough (& Focaccia) · 230*
food combining · 2, 3, 9
Four Seasons of Fruit Crisp · 247

**G**

garlic
Roasted Chickpeas with Garlic &
Chard · 200
Sausage & Chickpea Soup with Garlic
& Avocado · 128
Slow-Cooked Lamb Shanks with
Lentils, Garlic & Rosemary · 170
Spaghetti with Garlic, Chickpeas &
Braised Kale or Chard · 191
ginger
Apple, Sprouted Bean & Crystalized
Ginger Salad with Cambozola · 80
Ginger Chews · 242
Ginger Snaps · 241
Upside-Down Pear Gingerbread · 254
goat cheese
Roasted Beet Salad with Wild Rice,
Goat Cheese & Chickpeas · 87
grains (general)
cooking of (general) · 10
cooking of (specific to each
type) · 10–13
nutrients of · 2, 9
storing · 10
variety in the diet · 2, 10
varieties of · 5, 10–13
Granola · 37
Greek Salad with Chickpeas &
Bow-Ties · 84
green beans
Classic Three-Bean Salad · 79
Panzanella Salad · 93
Guinness Baked Beans · 201

**H**

Hoisin Black Bean Lettuce
Wraps · 52
Huevos Rancheros · 30
Hummus Five Ways · 40

**I**

Italian Threesome · 117
Italian Vegetable Stew · 116

**J**

Jamaican Red Beans & Rice · 163

**K**

kale
Black-Eyed Pea & Kale Soup with
Cheesy Croutons · 126
Spaghetti with Garlic, Chickpeas &
Braised Kale or Chard · 191
kidney beans
Beef & Barley Chili · 158
Cheesy Black Bean Dip · 50
Classic Three-Bean Salad · 79
Guinness Baked Beans · 201
Jamaican Red Beans & Rice · 163
Maple Baked Beans · 202
Mexican Fried Rice · 160
Pulled Pork & Beans · 156
Spinach, Bean & Pasta Soup · 136
Two-Bean & Sweet Potato Chipotle
Chili · 159

**L**

lamb
Lamb & Lentil Shepherd's Pie with
White Bean Mashed Potatoes · 174
Slow-Cooked Lamb Shanks with
Lentils, Garlic & Rosemary · 170
lasagna
Roasted Squash, Garlic, Mushroom &
White Bean Lasagna · 196
Lebanese Spinach & Lentil
Soup · 118
leeks
White Bean Vichyssoise (Potato &
Leek Soup) · 141
legumes (general)
baking with · 210
canned vs. dry · 3
cooking from dry · 6
definition of · 2
dry vs. cooked volumes · 3
economic considerations · 1, 3
environmental role · 1
fibre content of · 1, 2
flatulence · 3, 6
freezing · 3, 9
nutrients · 1, 2
protein · 1, 2, 3, 7
presoaking · 6
puréeing · 3, 210
quick-soaking · 8
salting during cooking · 8
shelf life · 1, 3, 6

role in world cuisines · 1, 3
varieties of · 2, 4
lemon
Citrus Bliss Pound Cake · 218
Rice or Orzo Salad with Chickpeas,
Spinach, Lemon & Feta · 78
Stir-Fried Chickpeas & Asparagus with
Brown Rice & Lemon Tahini
Dressing · 169
lentils (general) see legumes
lentils (recipes)
Baklava · 252
Butter Chicken & Lentils · 176
Candied Red Lentils and Lentil
Meal · 260
Chocolate Cupcakes · 211
Coconut Dal Curry · 151
Curried Dal Dip · 44
Curried Sweet Potato, Carrot & Red
Lentil Soup · 132
Easy Red Lentil Dal · 207
Four Seasons of Fruit Crisp · 247
Lamb & Lentil Shepherd's Pie with
White Bean Mashed Potatoes · 174
Lebanese Spinach & Lentil Soup · 118
Lentil & Barley Salad with Tomatoes,
Spinach & Feta · 71
Lentil & Mushroom Bourguignon · 154
Lentil & Walnut Burgers · 103
Lentil & Wild Rice Salad · 91
Lentils Braised in Red Wine · 206
Marinated Lentil Couscous Salad · 73
Marinated Roasted Eggplant, Pepper &
Mushrooms with Lentils · 54
Oatmeal Raisin Cookies · 237
Oatmeal Raisin Scones · 212
Morning Glory Muffins · 20
Palak Dal · 179
Poached Eggs over Warm Lentils with
Bacon · 167
Pumpkin Chocolate Chip Loaf
Cake · 215
Red Lentil & Sweet Potato Curry with
Spinach · 146
Red Lentil Pumpkin Pie · 258
Roasted Sausages with Braised
Lentils · 155
Roasted Tomato Soup with Red Lentils
& Steel-Cut Oats · 122
Samosas · 42
Sausage, Lentil & Barley Soup · 138

Index

Savoury Hand Pies with Sun-Dried
   Tomatoes, Lentils, Olives & Feta · 58
Slow-Cooked Lamb Shanks with
   Lentils, Garlic & Rosemary · 170
Soba Noodles with Mushroom & Lentil
   Cream Sauce · 192
Spanish Tortilla with Lentils · 35
Thick, Chewy Granola Bars · 250
Vegetable Lentil Curry · 150
lettuce wraps
   Hoisin Black Bean Lettuce Wraps · 52

## M

macaroni and cheese
   Baked Mac & Cheese with Little White
      Beans · 184
mango
   Curried Quinoa Salad with Black Beans
      & Mango · 66
Maple Baked Beans · 202
maple syrup
   Maple Baked Beans · 202
   Roasted Chickpeas & Pecans with Bacon
      & Maple Syrup · 32
Marinated Lentil Couscous
   Salad · 73
Marinated Roasted Eggplant,
   Pepper & Mushrooms with
   Lentils · 54
Mexican Fried Rice · 160
miso
   Cold Soba Noodles with Miso
      Dressing · 83
Minestrone · 119
Morning Glory Muffins · 20
muffins
   Cranberry Cornmeal Mini Muffins · 23
   Morning Glory Muffins · 20
Mulligatawny Soup · 115
mushrooms
   Brown Rice Pasta with Mushrooms,
      Prosciutto & Sprouted Beans · 193
   Creamy Mushroom Soup with Little
      White Beans · 113
   Lentil & Mushroom Bourguignon · 154
   Marinated Roasted Eggplant, Pepper &
      Mushroom with Lentils · 54
   Roasted Squash, Garlic, Mushroom &
      White Bean Lasagna · 196
   Soba Noodles with Mushroom & Lentil
      Cream Sauce · 192

## N

Naan · 223
navy beans see white beans
New-School Tuna Melts · 105
No-Knead Bread · 226
noodles see also pasta
   Cold Soba Noodles with Miso
      Dressing · 83
   Soba Noodles with Mushroom & Lentil
      Cream Sauce · 192
   Vietnamese Rice Paper Rolls · 62

## O

Oatmeal Raisin Cookies · 237
Oatmeal Raisin Scones · 212
oats
   about · 11
   Apricot-Almond Biscotti · 257
   Four Seasons of Fruit Crisp · 247
   Granola · 37
   Oatmeal Raisin Cookies · 237
   Oatmeal Raisin Scones · 212
   Roasted Tomato Soup with Red Lentils
      & Steel-Cut Oats · 122
   Thick, Chewy Granola Bars · 250
olives
   Savoury Hand Pies with Sun-Dried
      Tomatoes, Lentils, Olives &
      Feta · 58
   White Bean, Tomato & Olive
      Bruschetta · 57
one-dish meals
   Aloo Gobi with Chickpeas · 148
   Beef & Barley Chili · 158
   Butter Chicken & Lentils · 176
   Chana Masala · 145
   Chicken & Bean Braise · 180
   Coconut Dal Curry · 151
   Couscous with Roasted Vegetables,
      Feta & Chickpeas · 152
   Jamaican Red Beans & Rice · 163
   Lamb & Lentil Shepherd's Pie with
      White Bean Mashed Potatoes · 174
   Lentil & Mushroom
      Bourguignon · 154
   Mexican Fried Rice · 160
   Quick Chickpea Curry · 147
   Palak Dal · 179
   Poached Eggs over Warm Lentils
      with Bacon · 167
   Pulled Pork & Beans · 156
   Red Lentil & Sweet Potato Curry
      with Spinach · 146

Roasted Sausages with Braised
   Lentils · 155
Slow-Cooked Lamb Shanks with
   Lentils, Garlic & Rosemary · 170
Stir-Fried Chickpeas & Asparagus
   with Brown Rice & Lemon Tahini
   Dressing · 169
Thai Chicken Thighs with Black Beans
   & Sweet Potatoes · 173
Turkey & Black Bean Chili with
   Butternut Squash & Apples · 175
Two-Bean & Sweet Potato Chipotle
   Chili · 159
Vegetable Lentil Curry · 150
White Bean Risotto with Sun-
   Dried Tomatoes, Spinach &
   Parmesan · 165
onions
   Spaghetti Carbonara with Caramelized
      Onions & Peas · 189
oranges
   Citrus Bliss Pound Cake · 218

## P

Palak Dal · 179
Pancakes · 16
Panzanella Salad · 93
parmesan
   White Bean Risotto with Sun-
      Dried Tomatoes, Spinach &
      Parmesan · 165
parsnips
   Roasted Parsnip Soup · 120
pasta see also noodles
   Baked Mac & Cheese with Little White
      Beans · 184
   Baked Penne with Sausage, Spinach
      & Beans · 187
   Brown Rice Pasta with Mushrooms,
      Prosciutto & Sprouted Beans · 193
   Greek Salad with Chickpeas &
      Bow-Ties · 84
   Pasta e Fagioli (Fazool) · 188
   Rice or Orzo Salad with Chickpeas,
      Spinach, Lemon & Feta · 78
   Roasted Squash, Garlic, Mushroom &
      White Bean Lasagna · 196
   Spaghetti Cacio e Pepe e Fagioli · 194
   Spaghetti Carbonara with Caramelized
      Onions & Peas · 189
   Spaghetti with Garlic, Chickpeas &
      Braised Kale or Chard · 191

*Spilling the Beans*

Spaghetti with Sausage Meatballs,
Tomatoes & Little White Beans · 186
White Bean & Tuna Pasta Salad · 92
Pasta e Fagioli (Fazool) · 188
pastry · 58
peanut sauce · 62
pears
Upside-Down Pear Gingerbread · 254
peas, green
Spaghetti Carbonara with Caramelized
Onions & Peas · 189
pecans
Black Bean Brownies · 244
Pecan Brown Sugar Shortbread · 238
Roasted Chickpeas & Pecans with Bacon
& Maple Syrup · 32
peppers
Couscous with Roasted Vegetables, Feta
& Chickpeas · 152
Marinated Roasted Eggplant, Pepper &
Mushrooms with Lentils · 54
Roasted Red Pepper, Tomato & Black
Bean Soup · 134
pesto
Chicken & White Bean Stew with
Pesto · 139
pie
Red Lentil Pumpkin Pie · 258
Savoury Hand Pies with Sun-Dried
Tomatoes, Lentils, Olives & Feta · 58
pinto beans
Mexican Fried Rice · 160
Pasta e Fagioli (Fazool) · 188
pizza (and pizza dough)
No-Knead Bread · 226
Pizza Dough (& Focaccia) · 230
Sunny Side Up Breakfast Pizzas · 29
Pizza Dough (& Focaccia) · 230
Poached Eggs over Warm Lentils
with Bacon · 167
pork see also sausages
Brown Rice Pasta with Mushrooms,
Prosciutto & Sprouted Beans · 193
Poached Eggs over Warm Lentils with
Bacon · 167
Pulled Pork & Beans · 156
potatoes see also sweet potatoes
Aloo Gobi with Chickpeas · 148
Lamb & Lentil Shepherd's Pie with
White Bean Mashed Potatoes · 174
White Bean Mashed Potatoes · 203
White Bean Vichyssoise (Potato & Leek
Soup) · 141

Pretzels · 229
prosciutto
Brown Rice Pasta with Mushrooms,
Prosciutto & Sprouted Beans · 193
Pulled Pork & Beans · 156
pulses see legumes
pumpkin
Pumpkin Chocolate Chip Loaf
Cake · 215
Red Lentil Pumpkin Pie · 258

Q
quesadillas
Black Bean Quesadillas · 100
Quick Chickpea Curry · 147
quinoa
about · 11
Curried Quinoa Salad with Black Beans
& Mango · 66
Quinoa, Cauliflower, Chickpea & Feta
Sort-of-Slaw · 74

R
raisins
Oatmeal Raisin Cookies · 237
Oatmeal Raisin Scones · 212
Red Lentil & Sweet Potato Curry
with Spinach · 146
Red Lentil Pumpkin Pie · 258
refried beans
Crispy Black Bean Tacos with Feta &
Slaw · 98
how to make · 98
Huevos Rancheros · 30
rice
brown · 12
Brown & Wild Rice & Barley Salad with
Chickpeas · 72
Brown Rice Pasta with Mushrooms,
Prosciutto & Sprouted Beans · 193
Jamaican Red Beans & Rice · 163
Lentil & Wild Rice Salad · 91
Mexican Fried Rice · 160
Rice or Orzo Salad with Chickpeas,
Spinach, Lemon & Feta · 78
Roasted Beet Salad with Wild Rice,
Goat Cheese & Chickpeas · 87
Stir-Fried Chickpeas & Asparagus
with Brown Rice & Lemon Tahini
Dressing · 169

White Bean Risotto with Sun-
Dried Tomatoes, Spinach &
Parmesan · 165
wild · 13
rice paper
Vietnamese Rice Paper Rolls · 62
Roasted Beet Salad with Wild
Rice, Goat Cheese &
Chickpeas · 87
Roasted Chickpeas & Pecans with
Bacon & Maple Syrup · 32
Roasted Chickpeas with Garlic &
Chard · 200
Roasted Parsnip Soup · 120
Roasted Red Pepper, Tomato &
Black Bean Soup · 134
Roasted Sausages with Braised
Lentils · 155
Roasted Squash, Garlic,
Mushroom & White Bean
Lasagna · 196
Roasted Tomato Soup with
Red Lentils & Steel-Cut
Oats · 122
rosemary
Slow-Cooked Lamb Shanks with
Lentils, Garlic & Rosemary · 170

S
salads
Apple, Sprouted Bean & Crystalized
Ginger Salad with Cambozola · 80
Barley & Wheat Berry Salad with
Chickpeas & Feta · 69
Brown & Wild Rice & Barley Salad with
Chickpeas · 72
Charred Corn, Black Bean & Toasted
Barley Salad · 76
Classic Three-Bean Salad · 79
Cold Soba Noodles with Miso
Dressing · 83
Curried Quinoa Salad with Black Beans
& Mango · 66
Greek Salad with Chickpeas &
Bow-Ties · 84
Lentil & Barley Salad with Tomatoes,
Spinach & Feta · 71
Lentil & Wild Rice Salad · 91
Marinated Lentil Couscous Salad · 73
Panzanella Salad · 93
Quinoa, Cauliflower, Chickpea & Feta
Sort-of-Slaw · 74

Index

Rice or Orzo Salad with Chickpeas,
  Spinach, Lemon & Feta · 78
Roasted Beet Salad with Wild Rice,
  Goat Cheese & Chickpeas · 87
Spiced Couscous Salad with
  Chickpeas · 88
Tabbouleh with Barley &
  Chickpeas · 90
White Bean & Tuna Pasta Salad · 92
Samosas · 42
sandwiches
  Beet & Black Bean Burgers · 101
  Black Bean Quesadillas · 100
  Chickpea Masala Sandwiches
    (Doubles) · 106
  Crispy Black Bean Tacos with Feta &
    Slaw · 98
  Falafel · 96
  Lentil & Walnut Burgers · 103
  New-School Tuna Melts · 105
  Turkey Chickpea Sliders · 104
sausages
  Baked Penne with Sausage, Spinach
    & Beans · 187
  Chorizo, Black Bean & Corn
    Chowder · 131
  Italian Threesome · 117
  Italian Vegetable Stew · 116
  Mexican Fried Rice · 160
  Roasted Sausages with Braised
    Lentils · 155
  Sausage & Chickpea Soup with Garlic &
    Avocado · 128
  Sausage, Black Bean & Sweet Potato
    Soup · 135
  Sausage, Lentil & Barley Soup · 138
  Spaghetti with Sausage Meatballs,
    Tomatoes & Little White Beans · 186
Savoury Hand Pies with
  Sun-Dried Tomatoes,
  Lentils, Olives & Feta · 58
scones
  Oatmeal Raisin Scones · 212
Seafood Chowder · 125
shepherd's pie
  Lamb & Lentil Shepherd's Pie with
    White Bean Mashed Potatoes · 174
side dishes see beany sides
Slow-Cooked Lamb Shanks
  with Lentils, Garlic &
  Rosemary · 170
slow cooker, to cook dry beans · 9

soba noodles
  Cold Soba Noodles with Miso
    Dressing · 83
  Soba Noodles with Mushroom & Lentil
    Cream Sauce · 192
soups and stews
  Black Bean Soup · 112
  Black-Eyed Pea & Kale Soup with
    Cheesy Croutons · 126
  Chicken Noodle Soup · 110
  Chicken & White Bean Stew with
    Pesto · 139
  Chicken, White Bean, Corn & Cheddar
    Chowder · 130
  Chorizo, Black Bean & Corn
    Chowder · 131
  Creamy Mushroom Soup with Little
    White Beans · 113
  Curried Sweet Potato, Carrot & Red
    Lentil Soup · 132
  Italian Threesome · 117
  Italian Vegetable Stew · 116
  Lebanese Spinach & Lentil Soup · 118
  Minestrone · 119
  Mulligatawny Soup · 115
  Roasted Parsnip Soup · 120
  Roasted Red Pepper, Tomato & Black
    Bean Soup · 134
  Roasted Tomato Soup with Red Lentils
    & Steel-Cut Oats · 122
  Sausage & Chickpea Soup with Garlic &
    Avocado · 128
  Sausage, Black Bean & Sweet Potato
    Soup · 135
  Sausage, Lentil & Barley Soup · 138
  Seafood Chowder · 125
  Spinach, Bean & Pasta Soup · 136
  White Bean Vichyssoise (Potato & Leek
    Soup) · 141
spaghetti see also pasta
  Spaghetti Cacio e Pepe e Fagioli · 194
  Spaghetti Carbonara with
    Caramelized Onions & Peas · 189
  Spaghetti with Garlic,
    Chickpeas & Braised Kale or
    Chard · 191
  Spaghetti with Sausage Meatballs,
    Tomatoes & Little White Beans · 186
Spanish Tortilla with Lentils · 35
Spiced Couscous Salad with
  Chickpeas · 88
Spiced Roasted Chickpeas with
  Walnuts · 47

spinach
  Baked Penne with Sausage, Spinach &
    Beans · 187
  Lebanese Spinach & Lentil Soup · 118
  Lentil & Barley Salad with Tomatoes,
    Spinach & Feta · 71
  Palak Dal · 179
  Red Lentil & Sweet Potato Curry with
    Spinach · 146
  Rice or Orzo Salad with Chickpeas,
    Spinach, Lemon & Feta · 78
  Spinach & Artichoke Dip with White
    Beans · 60
  Spinach, Bean & Pasta Soup · 136
  White Bean Risotto with Sun-Dried
    Tomatoes, Spinach &
    Parmesan · 165
sprouted beans
  Apple, Sprouted Bean & Crystalized
    Ginger Salad with Cambozola · 80
  Brown Rice Pasta with Mushrooms,
    Prosciutto & Sprouted Beans · 193
  Cold Soba Noodles with Miso
    Dressing · 83
  Vietnamese Rice Paper Rolls · 62
squash
  Roasted Squash, Garlic, Mushroom &
    White Bean Lasagna · 196
  Turkey & Black Bean Chili with
    Butternut Squash & Apples · 175
stews see soups and stews
Sticky Cinnamon Buns · 24
Stir-Fried Chickpeas &
  Asparagus with Brown
  Rice & Lemon Tahini
  Dressing · 169
Sunny Side Up Breakfast
  Pizzas · 29
sweet potatoes see also potatoes
  Aloo Gobi with Chickpeas · 148
  Chard, White Bean & Sweet Potato
    Gratin · 205
  Couscous with Roasted Vegetables, Feta
    & Chickpeas · 152
  Curried Sweet Potato, Carrot & Red
    Lentil Soup · 132
  Red Lentil & Sweet Potato Curry with
    Spinach · 146
  Sausage, Black Bean & Sweet Potato
    Soup · 135
  Thai Chicken Thighs with Black Beans
    & Sweet Potatoes · 173
  Two-Bean & Sweet Potato Chipotle
    Chili · 159

**T**

Tabbouleh with Barley & Chickpeas · 90
tacos
Crispy Black Bean Tacos with Feta & Slaw · 98
tahini
Stir-Fried Chickpeas & Asparagus with Brown Rice & Lemon Tahini Dressing · 169
Thai Chicken Thighs with Black Beans & Sweet Potatoes · 173
Thick, Chewy Granola Bars · 250
three-bean salad
Classic Three-Bean Salad · 79
tomatoes
Lentil & Barley Salad with Tomatoes, Spinach & Feta · 71
Roasted Red Pepper, Tomato & Black Bean Soup · 134
Roasted Tomato Soup with Red Lentils & Steel-Cut Oats · 122
Savoury Hand Pies with Sun-Dried Tomatoes, Lentils, Olives & Feta · 58
Spaghetti with Sausage Meatballs, Tomatoes & Little White Beans · 186
White Bean, Tomato & Olive Bruschetta · 57
White Bean Risotto with Sun-Dried Tomatoes, Spinach & Parmesan · 165
tortillas
Spanish Tortilla with Lentils · 35
tuna see fish
turkey
Chorizo, Black Bean & Corn Chowder · 131
Turkey & Black Bean Chili with Butternut Squash & Apples · 175
Turkey Chickpea Sliders · 104
Two-Bean & Sweet Potato Chipotle Chili · 159

**U**

Upside-Down Pear Gingerbread · 254

**V**

Vegetable Lentil Curry · 150
Vietnamese Rice Paper Rolls · 62

**W**

waffles
Buttermilk Waffles · 18
walnuts
Baklava · 252
Edamame or Broad Bean & Walnut Dip · 45
Lentil & Walnut Burgers · 103
Spiced Roasted Chickpeas with Walnuts · 47
wheat berries
about · 12
Barley & Wheat Berry Salad with Chickpeas & Feta · 69
Wheat Thins · 233
white beans
Apricot-Almond Biscotti · 257
Antipasto · 49
Baked Mac & Cheese with Little White Beans · 184
Baked Penne with Sausage, Spinach & Beans · 187
Banana Bread · 216
Blueberry Big Crumb Cake · 220
Brioche Burger or Slider Buns · 224
Buttermilk Waffles · 18
Carrot Cake · 222
Chard, White Bean & Sweet Potato Gratin · 205
Chicken & Bean Braise · 180
Chicken & White Bean Stew with Pesto · 139
Chicken Noodle Soup · 110
Chicken, White Bean, Corn & Cheddar Chowder · 130
Chocolate Crisps · 240
Chocolate Cupcakes · 211
Citrus Bliss Pound Cake · 218
Creamy Mushroom Soup with Little White Beans · 113
Ginger Chews · 242
Ginger Snaps · 241
Guinness Baked Beans · 201
Italian Threesome · 117
Lamb & Lentil Shepherd's Pie with White Bean Mashed Potatoes · 174
Maple Baked Beans · 202
Naan · 223
New-School Tuna Melts · 105
No-Knead Bread · 226
Pancakes · 16
Panzanella Salad · 93
Pasta e Fagioli (Fazool) · 188
Pecan Brown Sugar Shortbread · 238
Pizza Dough (& Focaccia) · 230
Pretzels · 229
Roasted Parsnip Soup · 120
Roasted Squash, Garlic, Mushroom & White Bean Lasagna · 196
Seafood Chowder · 125
Spaghetti Cacio e Pepe e Fagioli · 194
Spaghetti Carbonara with Caramelized Onions & Peas · 189
Spaghetti with Sausage Meatballs, Tomatoes & Little White Beans · 186
Spinach & Artichoke Dip with White Beans · 60
Sticky Cinnamon Buns · 24
Sunny Side Up Breakfast Pizzas · 29
Upside-Down Pear Gingerbread · 254
Wheat Thins · 233
White Bean & Tuna Pasta Salad · 92
White Bean Mashed Potatoes · 203
White Bean Risotto with Sun-Dried Tomatoes, Spinach & Parmesan 165
White Bean, Tomato & Olive Bruschetta · 57
White Bean Vichyssoise (Potato & Leek Soup) · 141
Yeasted Banana Bread with Cardamom · 234
wild rice see rice
wine
Lentils Braised in Red Wine · 206

**Y**

Yeasted Banana Bread with Cardamom · 234
yellow wax beans
Classic Three-Bean Salad · 79

**Z**

Zucchini Bread · 217

Index

268